Lessons From The Mountain

The Mountain

Rebecca Hendrickson

LESSONS FROM THE MOUNTAIN
Published in the United States of America
By Artemis Publishing Company
P.O. Box 633
Springfield, Tennessee 37172 USA
https://www.artemispublishingco.com

Copyright 2020 by Rebecca Hendrickson
ISBN: 978-1-7354197-0-1

This is a work of fiction. Except for historical and famous characters, all characters, names, places, and events appearing in this work are a product of the author's imagination or used fictitiously. Any resemblance to real persons, living or dead, is entirely co-incidental.

Annie

Freezing, yet soaked in her own sweat, the goosebumps covered her body once again. It wasn't like the night sweats that happened after she first had Avery, or Nicholas, for that matter. This time it felt like she had a fever, but she knew she wasn't sick. She wanted to get out of bed and change her shirt, but she couldn't move her legs. They felt like logs with little ants crawling all over them that would creep in the holes if she moved too quickly. She felt nauseous, and she knew that as soon as she stood up she was going to dry heave in the bathroom like she had the last two mornings. Two rocks sat on top of her chest, filled with milk that wasn't going to anyone even though she had been weaning for two weeks.

She had only opened her eyes for a moment. It was too bright in the room. Michael had put shades over the skylights on the ceiling, but it still pained her eyes to have them open. Even the clock was too bright as she glanced at it quickly, the red numbers seeming to jump off the black background towards her. She had turned to lay on her back, the popcorn ceiling the last image she saw. God, she hated the popcorn ceilings—the unevenness of the surface, the rough texture. Everything in her room bothered her.

Nicholas was going to be in her room any minute and she would have to pretend he had just woken her up out of a peaceful slumber. She would have to put a smile on her face and pretend to tickle his belly, and let him climb into the bed if he wanted to give her a hug before the morning tantrums began with Dad. Avery was only six weeks old, but she had been sleeping through the night since she was four weeks. She didn't know babies like her who just slept and were peaceful all day and night. Nicholas hadn't been difficult, but he had been up every three hours like she had been told would be the case with a newborn baby.

She should be well-rested and ready for playtime with Nicholas, but Annie had been awake most of the night. She had spent hours restlessly tossing and turning, looking at the clock panicking about how tired she was going to be the next day, anxious that she was unable to sleep when everything was conducive to slumber. The noise machine whirred, the lights were off, and her husband slept silently next to her on one side while Avery peacefully slept in the bassinet attached to her bed.

She had experienced some hormonal insomnia after both children the first week home from the hospital, that mix of adrenaline with having just birthed a baby and the slight panic that she now had to keep the tiny human alive. Wondering if she was really qualified for such responsibility was familiar, and she knew it would be over once her milk came in. That had faded after the first couple of days as she settled into having the baby home and the oxytocin began to course through her blood. She had finally fallen asleep around four in the morning, feeling the familiar dread she felt anticipating the morning.

This wasn't supposed to happen. She had resumed her Paxil only days after Avery was born. She went through postpartum depression after Nicholas, so she had already taken the preventative measures to make sure it didn't happen again. With Nicholas, she had to wait months for the medicine to kick in, so this time she would just take it before any symptoms began. There was no way she was going to allow herself to lose time with her children again.

Breastfeeding hadn't worked very well with either of her children. She had an inverted nipple that neither could latch on to. Angus, the name she had given her nipple in the tenth grade after watching the film about the overweight child and seeing his nipples when he went to jump in the pool, was impossible for either child to feed from without assistance. That was what Annie had sitting on her left breast, and it had always been a joke among her closest friends. She used nipple shields, went to lactation consultants, but with both of her children, breastfeeding was a failure. She pumped as much as she could, but she never made enough milk for her babies to gain weight. This stress she experienced with breastfeeding, coupled with the fact that it took her children over an hour to drain her breasts, only to have the doctor tell her they weren't gaining enough, led her to supplement with formula. With Nicholas, she had great guilt doing this. She was convinced she was lowering his IQ and leading him to a life of illnesses he wouldn't fight off, but he turned out to surpass all milestones, and when fourteen children in his preschool classroom got the flu, he was one of two who didn't. She wondered if the other was formula-fed too. She knew four weeks after Avery's birth that she was done breastfeeding her too.

When she stopped breastfeeding with Nicholas, she was suddenly sick every day. She was vomiting and having diarrhea, unable to eat anything. She couldn't sleep at night and developed extreme anxiety over going to bed knowing that she wasn't going to be able to sleep and worrying about how tired she'd feel the next day. Her body was in a state of extreme agitation and none of the doctors were listening to her. She was dying. She had just had a beautiful baby that she brought into this world, and now she had a terminal illness.

She went to doctor after doctor, and all of them were convinced that she just had Irritable Bowel Syndrome, or some stomach bug that wouldn't go away. She had mastitis at one point and had to take two different kinds of antibiotics to make it go away, so one doctor hypothesized that it must be a bacterial infection from too many antibiotics. She had to poop into a bag to send to a lab to be tested, and her gynecologist's best advice was to buy some Boost, so she didn't lose so much weight. She was beyond losing the weight she had gained from the pregnancy and her old clothes were falling off of her body. She was already a slim person, a size four in most stores, and her doctor was worried that she was losing too much weight too quickly, but he had no answers for her.

When she knew she couldn't take care of Nicholas alone, she had reached out to her mother and father. They had immediately come to visit, her father bringing her a few of his Ativan to help her get some rest while they watched the baby. Don, her father, was an endocrinologist. He had been sure that she was experiencing something hormonal and wrote her out exactly what to say to the doctors and what to ask for. They didn't complete any of the tests he recommended and just shrugged her off as a hypochondriac who had contracted a stomach virus, was overwhelmed with being a new mom, and had no coping skills. Annie never questioned why her father had an entire bottle of Ativan he could part with knowing that he was still taking it on a daily basis.

Annie finally found a primary care doctor who she hoped would figure out her illness and point her in the right direction. The doctor took one look at her and asked, "Are you feeling anxious or depressed?"

Annie immediately burst into tears. "Of course, I'm anxious and depressed," she cried. "I just had this beautiful baby and I can't enjoy him because I'm sick all of the time and can't sleep. I go to bed every night afraid of staying up all night and terrified that I won't make it through the next day and be able to parent." She even told the doctor of instances where she had been giving Nicholas a bottle and had to throw up into her own hands because she couldn't get up and run to the bathroom.

The doctor asked, "Have you ever taken medication before?"

"I had been on Paxil for a couple of years before having Nicholas"

"Maybe it's time to try that again. You might be experiencing postpartum depression. That's what this sounds like."

Annie was truly offended. Postpartum depression? She loved her child. He was the only thing that was keeping her going. "I do not have postpartum depression," she stated firmly.

The doctor ignored her protest and tried to avoid the confrontation. "Then maybe you'd like to try getting back on your medicine just to ease your anxiety and help you sleep. I can also prescribe a medication, Hydroxyzine, to help you sleep at night."

Annie, desperate to experience any relief, agreed to get back on her medication. It took months, but eventually Annie went back to her old self. Fortunately,

Nicholas was born in March, and Annie was a teacher. She was an English teacher at a middle school in a small town outside of Albany, New York called Niskayuna. Nicholas had been breastfed much longer than Avery, so Annie's illness didn't begin until the beginning of the summer, but she had the remainder of the summer to get back to feeling like a person again. It was a long summer filled with many tears, sleepless nights, and little eating, but by the time the school year started, Annie was able to function like a human.

After learning more from her doctor about postpartum depression, she learned that she had experienced an episode. She was able to accept it once she had returned to being the mother she knew she really was. It was purely hormonal and had nothing to do with her loving or not loving her child. When it was time to have Avery, she worried greatly about going through this again. She discussed it with her doctor and Nicholas's pediatrician to be sure that she had a plan after Avery was born, so she never had to go through it again. Her gynecologist assured her that every pregnancy was different, so just because she went through it with Nicholas, did not mean that she would go through it with Avery. The pediatrician gave her a list of medications that were safe to take while breastfeeding. Neither had really helped her develop a plan of action to make sure that she didn't lose months of her child's life again.

There she was, paralyzed in her bed, exhausted, yet so agitated she felt like she could get up and run a marathon. If she stayed completely still in one position, her stomach felt normal, but the minute she moved she felt like she was going to throw up. Since she hadn't eaten in days, she knew it would be nothing again. She was depressed again, and she knew this was what it was, but she was already on medication. She had been on the medication for a month, so it was possible it still needed more time to kick in, but how many more mornings could she wake up like this? She knew what lay ahead for the day, but before her mind could begin playing the tape of all she would have to get through just to have another night like she'd just had, she heard the pitter-patter of little feet.

"Mommy!" Nicholas burst into the room as Annie put her finger to her mouth and gestured towards Avery, still sound asleep in her swaddle. He was still in his pajamas and smelled like apple juice from breakfast and baby laundry soap since Annie was using it on everyone's clothes.

"Good morning sweetheart," She spoke softly as she pulled him into her bed, swallowing the bile that was coming up in her throat.

"Daddy, can I stay in Mommy's bed with her while you get ready for work?"

"Yes buddy, but remember, you have to pick out your clothes quickly and get ready to leave if I let you hang out," Michael warned him.

"Mommy, can we listen to Laurie?"

"Sure," Annie replied as she turned on the Laurie Berkner radio on her phone and slowly watched Avery's eyes open as she began to cry for her bottle. Annie reached over and made the bottle of formula that she had prepped for the night before. She sat in bed surrounded by both of her beautiful children, but she couldn't enjoy the moment. When Michael was done brushing his teeth and packing his lunch, Nicholas was going to throw a tantrum about getting dressed. Michael was going to storm into the room saying he couldn't take it anymore, and Annie would watch from the bed while feeding Avery as Michael carried a screaming Nicholas down the stairs and out the door to daycare. She already felt guilty for sending Nicholas to daycare even though she was home, but as part of her plan to prepare for Avery, she had decided she would send him until she felt back to herself hoping it would be sooner rather than later.

As Annie turned off Laurie Berkner, it was just as she expected. Nicholas refused to pick a pair of sweatpants that were all the same and all his favorite. Michael came into the bedroom pulling his hair back, turning red, and breathing heavily. Eventually, Michael forcefully put pants on Nicholas and carried him down the stairs of their condominium while she was still in bed giving Avery her bottle. She had hidden it again and gotten away with it. She leaned back onto the wall behind her bed closing her eyes and sighed. Michael was too focused on the stressors of the morning routine and going to work full time at a job he hated to notice anything different about his wife. She had pulled off her smile to Nicholas and pulled it together enough to give him the cuddles and tickles he looked forward to each morning. Deep down she knew that they would be paying for daycare much longer than they had intended, and she was unsure how much longer she was going to be able to keep this to herself. Her first confidante was usually her mother, but Winnie had so much going on with her father, that she couldn't fathom putting this on her too. This time, they wouldn't be able to come to her rescue. She finished the bottle and stood up to change Avery, but before she could get to the changing table, she had to drop her in the bassinet and run to throw up yellow water into the toilet.

Cade

It was the closest she had ever come to living in a trailer park. She spent almost twelve hours there each day. She got out of her car in the rocky parking lot, and headed onto the cement walkway past the third and fourth grade trailer. Her eyes looked away from the playground that sat in front of her trailer because she always found it so depressing. A metal swing set missing the swings with only a horizontal ladder to hang from was the school's sorry excuse for a play structure. The rest of the playground was light dirt with patches of grass no larger than frisbees. The sandbox was at the end of her porch with broken trucks and buckets to build sandcastles. She put her key into the lock of her half of the doublewide trailer and walked into her first-grade classroom.

There were no desks in her room, only a few large tables with chairs. Everything she had learned in graduate school about Smartboards was fruitless because her classroom didn't even have a projector. It had an old-fashioned chalkboard and a standing whiteboard easel that she only had because she had spent the classroom budget on it. With the two hundred dollars the school had given her to spend, she had spent most of it on the easel knowing she would need to use that the most after she had seen the resources available to her. There were four desktop computers, and none at her own desk. She tried to use them as part of her reading centers, but most of the time, the internet didn't work. She didn't need to use the computers too often, anyway, because nothing at the school was done through email. Most of the parents didn't have their own computers, so the only way she could reach any of them was by phone, and sometimes even those were disconnected. She had spruced up the room with a homemade bulletin board, using her own money to pay for the borders and background paper.

There had been no materials for her to use except math workbooks and a box of phonics materials from the only two programs the school purchased. Everything else had to be made by her. She had turned her classroom into her ideal learning environment given what she had. There were stations around the room for learning games she had purchased with her own money or created by hand, a library corner full of bean bags she had bought for the students to read alone or with partners, a listening center she had created out of her own tape recorder and library books, and a rolling cart of art supplies, so she could have students engage in projects both inside and outside. She had made her own posters, visited the teacher store frequently, and transformed her trailer into the closest she could get to a typical first grade classroom given the circumstances.

But the trailer was never the right temperature, as the heat or air conditioner were always turned off at night to save money, so she either walked into a trailer full of steam or one that felt like a refrigerator. It was another reason why she came in an hour early each morning. She went to her bathroom—at least she had her own bathroom. Not many teachers could say that about their classrooms. She turned on the water and splashed her face trying to wake herself up. This was how she always felt by Fridays. It was like she was in the army, running drills all day until she was completely worn down. She had drunk her coffee on the hour commute from Raleigh into the countryside, but she was exhausted.

There was still an hour until the students would arrive. Every day, she came in an hour early and stayed at least two hours after the students left organizing for the following day. She had to. There were only twenty minutes a day for her to prepare anything for the class and teaching first grade required a lot of preparation. Maybe she was just overwhelmed with everything that was going on with her mother and father, or maybe she just questioned whether she had the energy to get through another day in the classroom, but Cade felt like getting back in her car and driving the hour back to Raleigh. She fantasized about crawling into bed, binge-watching television on the couch, and letting her mind go blank for the first time since the school year started. In reality, Cade hadn't taken one day off the whole year, not even when she was sick. The idea of telling someone else how to make it through her day was more daunting than coming in sick.

Cade had taken the job because there was nothing else. Rochester, New York, where she had gone to graduate school had been too cold, and she didn't want to go back home to Norwalk, Connecticut. She was determined to set out on her own adventure somewhere warm. She would live in an up and coming city in the South and start a new life hoping her boyfriend followed her when he finished his degree. Ryan was getting his doctorate, so he would be done at the end of the school year, and he promised he was going to move to North Carolina with her. They had only been dating for a few months, but their love had been immediate and strong. He was set to graduate in May, and he said he would join her as soon as he was done. She had applied to forty-four jobs and heard from one. This one.

When she came for her interview, Cade had flown out by herself, with the help of her parents' finances, rented herself a car for the first time in her adult life, and drove an hour outside of Raleigh into the middle of nowhere. On her way, she passed nothing except farms and trailer parks advertising that they had sewage and running water. When she got to the town, she looked around for a place to grab some food since she was early for her interview and hungry. All that was there were fast food restaurants and a dollar store. She pulled into the Subway and got herself a sandwich. Her stomach was filled with butterflies and after two bites of her sandwich, she decided to go drive and see the school. She could pull over somewhere else to finish later.

Cade drove her rental past a trailer park and couldn't find the school. Had her GPS been mistaken? She drove back and forth on the street looking for a school that might be hidden until she saw the sign. A small wooden sign with Blue River Charter School hung just like a Coldwell Banker sign on a house for sale. There wasn't exactly a place to park, so she assumed that the open lot of rocks was where her car belonged. From her car, she stared at the "school" in awe. There was no building. It was only a small town of double-wide trailers with cement walkways connecting them. There were no decorations, and the only feature indicating she was somewhere other than the homes of people living in town was a sign that read "Main Office" and pointed to the trailer furthest to the right. Cade pulled right out and parked her car at the nearest pharmacy.

"I can't even go in. I wasted your money. This was a complete waste of my time," Cade called her mother on the verge of tears. "The website looked like any school website. Mom, it's a trailer park!"

"Well, you're already there," Winnie had replied. "You may as well go and see the school. You were drawn to it for some reason."

It was true. Cade had been excited about the school. It was an inclusive, project-based learning school. She had just finished her master's degree at a progressive school that promoted exactly what this school claimed as their values.

During the interview, the principal, Ms. Jay, had clearly read over her resume as she had highlighted what she liked about Cade. The front office staff was friendly and made jokes with other staff members as they came in asking for favors and were met with sarcastic, yet warm responses. Ms. Jay didn't interview her; they engaged in a passionate conversation about education. They held the same philosophies, and although the pay was going to be barely enough to live on and the commute would be long if she decided to stay in Raleigh, she would get to carry out exactly what she had learned in college. Her sisters were always complaining about how their souls had been crushed, there was too much bureaucracy, and everything was about the standardized test score in the schools where they taught. Here, at Blue River, it was about the child and what they needed. It was clearly a Title 1 school that didn't even have a building, but the students thrived there. In the surrounding schools, most had a literacy rate of lower than thirty percent, but Blue River's students passed state reading exams with an eighty percent success rate. What Cade didn't learn in the interview was that in order to make this possible, teachers had to give their hearts, souls, and every ounce of free time.

"Teaching is hard. Do you know how hard teaching is?" was the first question the woman who became her faculty advisor asked at her graduate school interview.

"Right, of course, it's an incredibly challenging job"

"No, but it's really hard. People don't realize how hard it is when they are getting into the field."

Cade hadn't really known what to say. Was she supposed to get up and leave? "I'm up for the challenge," she had assured her advisor.

"And if you ever think you are done, then it's time to quit," she had been told.

It turned out her mentor had been right. Teaching was ridiculously hard, especially at Blue River. Cade spent the entire summer before school started making the classroom into her own. She had spent two thousand dollars of her own money buying books from thrift stores, materials to make activities for her reading centers, and she had spent hours researching project-based units to put together for her soon-to-be first class of first graders. The classroom only had basal readers, which Ms. Jay had told her she shouldn't be using, but they didn't have money for anything else. These were the *Dick and Jane* - type readers with no real stories, nothing that got kids excited about reading. She filled her classroom library with sets of books of all different levels. She made decorations, games out of shower curtains, file folder activities to learn phonics, egg carton games, anything she could put together for the kids she was so excited to meet.

It was, in some ways, a teacher's dream job. She had complete autonomy. Although there were assessments to track student progress, how she got her students there was up to her. She was the only first grade teacher. Each teacher had half of a double wide trailer for their classroom and there was only one class per grade capped at twenty-two students. As the school was inclusive, her room would be filled with students from all walks of life, different abilities, socioeconomic situations, and cultures. Students came from many different areas, and there were some students who traveled an hour from other rural towns just to attend this school that looked like what most of the students went home to at night. She had read about what strategies were needed to reach diverse learners. All of her research papers had earned an A, and she understood the philosophies that she needed to hold dear to her heart as the school year began. She had set up her classroom perfectly with everything she believed was needed to produce young, curious learners, readers, writers, and mathematicians.

The first day of school began with a student, Hunter, filling her toilet with all of the paper towels in the bathroom and attempting to stuff them down the toilet. They had to spend the rest of the day disrupting the kindergarten teacher every time they had to use the bathroom. First graders use the bathroom a lot. The school followed a discipline program that Cade fully supported where the students had to reflect on their behavior by drawing a picture of what they had done and have it signed by their parents. Hunter refused. He sat through the day in the corner looking at the paper missing all of her get-to-know-you activities she had put together with excitement, sure they would all be a family of learners by the end of the day.

By recess, Hunter finally filled out his reflection sheet. He went to hand it to Cade. "How old you is?" he asked in his southern drawl.

"I'm twenty-four."

"My ma's younger than you and she likes her boyfriends better than me"

Cade immediately knew it was going to take more than a library of books, homemade games, and a graduate education to teach at Blue River. It was also all she had to think about since she had moved so far away from her home in Connecticut. When she first moved down, she had lived with roommates she met on Craigslist and they had instantly become friends. They had shared some Facebook friends in common, so she was sure they weren't serial killers. It was a group of girls who had just graduated from North Carolina State University. Fortunately for her, they all decided to stay in Raleigh to work, so when she finally moved to her own place, she had friends to hang out with on the weekends. However, when she wasn't hanging out with her new friends, she was thinking about work. All of the time she thought about her students and what more she should be doing.

Cade was also sure she was going to get fired. She had great difficulty not receiving constant feedback like she had in school. Like a typical millennial, she wanted constant reassurance that she was doing okay, but as a teacher, much went unappreciated. There was so much work behind the scenes that never received feedback. Teachers usually only got observed a few times a year, and usually only heard from their bosses when there was a complaint. Cade found that this left her very unsettled most days, always worried that she was an incompetent teacher.

There were two students with autism in her class and neither one was learning to read the way she had hoped. One of them required an aide and spent much of the day screaming between transitions. He had been in a classroom designed for students exclusively with autism in the public schools, but Blue River included everyone, so he had been thrown into her regular first grade classroom. The special education teacher at the school offered minimal help, and wouldn't even let her see the students' Individualized Education Plans. She learned early on that this was because they were all out of compliance, and she hadn't been doing her job. Cade was on her own to meet the needs of everyone and it was taking its toll.

She turned on the air conditioner since it was a warm March day in North Carolina, and she began her day. She set up all of her centers, prepared for morning meeting, set up supplies for the science experiment of the day, and had each second of the day thought out and prepared because there would be no time once the first student walked through the door to get anything ready. In the twenty minutes she was given while the students had their one special (either computer or physical education), she typically used that time to go to the bathroom and walk to the copy machine. At least it wasn't supposed to rain, so she didn't need to cover her copies with an umbrella as she walked outside to the main office trailer.

Her teaching assistant would be there shortly to help in the small time she had her before she had to go to all of the other classrooms. She would empty the homework folders, fill them for the following night, collect any book orders, and most importantly, set the students up for lunch. Lunch was the worst time of the day at Blue River Charter School because there was no cafeteria. Not even during lunch did Cade have a minute to herself, not even to use the bathroom. The students ate lunch in the classroom, and it was her job to set this up for all of the first graders in the room. The trailer was equipped with a microwave and students were allowed to bring in meals that required only one minute to heat up. Since there were twenty-two students in the class, even if only half brought in their lunch, this meant she was spending most of her lunch eating by the microwave passing out lunches. Many students were on free and reduced lunch and received lunch from a local cafe in town. The teaching assistant had to deliver all of these to the students at the start of lunch, so Cade would have to wait while those who had nothing to eat kept themselves out of trouble and stayed in their seats as she organized lunch. She had a strict routine, but first graders were not known for their ability to sit still and quietly. Cade had set a rule that for the first ten minutes of lunch the class would listen to music and be silent, but lunch alone felt like a full day of work.

The hour commute was not helpful for Cade who had difficulty turning off her thoughts. It gave her too much time to think about what she would have to do all day and get nervous that she wouldn't be good enough. The views of the cornfields left her only to her own thoughts without any distractions as she thought about her mother, Winnie, and her father, Don, and all they were going through at home. Don had just come home, and she couldn't tell how Winnie was handling it. When they got on the phone on her commute home, she tended to be too wired from the day telling her mother all of the stories from school, her questions to Winnie about her life only an afterthought. In some ways, being so far away helped her to compartmentalize all that was going on with her family. However, her thoughts tended to roam to memories of the past two years with her father that she couldn't quite shake on her commutes into work. These thoughts were quickly disrupted as she heard the pounding of feet of her first student of the day. His dad taught seventh grade at the school, so he was always first.

In came Jack like a tornado. His medication hadn't yet kicked in. "What are we doing? What's the morning work today? What's the plan? Oh! Our math workbooks? Page forty-three? I hope I get to do the weather today!" He literally bounced into the chalkboard as he looked at the schedule and answered his own questions while Cade stayed silent, letting him slowly calm down. It was usually within minutes of the morning that he transformed from the Tasmanian Devil to a well-behaved, extremely bright child.

Next to come in was Evan. Evan had autism, but did not have an aide with him during the day. He threw his backpack on the floor and declared, "I have to go to the bathroom, but I am not going to spend the whole morning in there because I do NOT want to have to do my morning work during recess."

Cade chuckled to herself and her adrenaline began to take over her exhaustion. Mary came in wearing six of her mother's bras underneath her clothing. Cade could see them puffing out from her shirt as they were just dangling from her arms unclipped. "I'm wearing my ma's bras, wanna see?"

Cade had to cover her mouth to keep from laughing aloud. "No, Mary, let's keep our shirt down," she said, pursing her lips to hold in the laughter. She knew what would get her through the day: them.

Rye

The recorder seemed far away on the table, or maybe it was because there were so many people sitting around one table in the conference room. The conference room was usually freezing, but this time, Rye was sweating. The chairs around the table were all mismatched, but the lawyer had taken the nicest one they had, the one that could roll around the room if there weren't so many people crowding the space. Rye propped up in her seat and bent over the table aiming her voice towards the recorder and the lawyer who sat there scowling as she spoke. "This is adding fractions." Rye held up the paper where she had written out a fraction addition problem, "and this is mixed numbers." She held up the other sheet of paper with a mixed number problem clearly written out for a woman in her mid-forties. They had been going back and forth over this for thirty minutes in the meeting as the lawyer accused her of writing the same objective for Tommy as she had written the previous year.

Rye had felt compassion for Tommy's mother prior to this meeting, and knew she still would once it was over, but at the current moment she was ready to get up and leave. She couldn't fathom having to worry about her daughters if one was in his shoes. Tommy had a traumatic brain injury that caused seizures and greatly impacted the functioning of his frontal lobe. Against all odds, Tommy was a walking, reading, sensitive child who was a joy to talk with about topics of his own interest, but his frontal lobe was damaged. There was a point at which Rye could not change certain aspects about him, not to mention he had begun having mini seizures again which had caused him to spend weeks throughout the year monitored by neurosurgeons in a hospital. He couldn't pay attention to a lecture, he couldn't write without significant assistance to organize his ideas, he couldn't understand character perspectives or often those of other people, and his executive function was extremely impaired. However, Rye had taught him how to add fractions and she'd be damned if she let this lawyer say she hadn't.

All of Tommy's meetings came with a lawyer present, as did the meetings of many other students she worked with, so she should have been used to it at this point. She was used to having to defend herself to people who knew nothing about education, and who were hired for a hefty sum by families, so they had to prove they were worth their fee. However, this time, she had lost her patience. While she was in this meeting with the lawyers, so was a speech therapist, an occupational therapist, a psychologist, a counselor, and a science teacher all wasting thirty minutes of precious time that could be spent with students while a lawyer argued with her about the difference between fractions and mixed numbers. This was only the discussion about one objective. Rye knew they would be sitting there for hours more as each word written on his Individualized Education Plan was scrutinized. It took everything inside her not to roll her eyes and give the parents a dirty look. She had established a relationship with these parents; shouldn't they be defending her too? Didn't they realize how many resources were being spent on just one child—one who had defied all odds and was basically a walking miracle?

She kept herself calm by picturing herself in Tommy's mother's shoes. Wouldn't she do anything to advocate for either of her girls if they were in his position? If they were doing better than any doctor had expected, wouldn't she then hold onto hope that they could be doing even more? She sat back down in her seat and they moved on to the next objective.

Rye was the only daughter who had decided to stay home in Connecticut near her family in Norwalk. She worked in Fairfield County as a special education teacher teaching middle school students just like her sister Annie, only their experiences were so drastically different. It wasn't something they tended to bond over. Maybe it was because none of the girls had received special education services when they were younger, but she did not remember Norwalk being this litigious. Although the town where she worked was significantly wealthier, she couldn't fathom how just one town over, teachers were spending their time speaking to lawyers (and keeping data binders inches thick because every year they were asked to produce it by some parent who requested a record) instead of focusing on actually teaching children.

Maybe Rye had lost her empathy for some of the parents she worked with who expected perfection and miracles from her after what she had gone through over the last two years. Those who paid two hundred and fifty dollars an hour for an advocate to dissect every word she typed that she had already analyzed herself had begun to irk her more than usual. She could typically laugh it off with her coworkers, and by the time she got in her car in the afternoons she was over it, but this year it seemed to be bothering her more than usual. She had become frustrated with "the system," and not just the education system, but the health care system, the mental health system, and all of the systems that were designed to help people, but she had learned did not always do so. She had become like some of the parents who felt the need to hire these lawyers and advocates because it could feel like everyone was out to get you instead of help you, and she was losing her tolerance for being a part of it.

Since she was the closest to home, Rye had witnessed firsthand all that Winnie and Don had gone through over the past two years. She had visited the mental hospitals regularly, sat with her mother in the emergency room, watched her father being taken by the police. Each time she had to put her complete faith in these systems that she'd been told were there to help people, but every time they made situations worse. Her mother had become like some of the parents she worked with, defensive and guarded.

Tommy's meeting continued on for another three hours as the lawyers questioned everyone sitting around the table. He was fifteen years old and in the seventh grade, yet he still couldn't change his own clothes for gym. If he wore a button-down shirt, he would come into school with the buttons in the wrong hole, one side of the shirt hanging down much longer than the other. Rye often brought him into her room to help him fix it before the other kids could see. Tommy only had one family friend who was much older than he was, but he couldn't be trusted to go downtown with him and remember to look both ways before crossing the street. He also didn't understand his sarcasm and regularly got angry with him for what he had meant as jokes. The friendship was all he had, but was also one where he was taken on like a younger brother, rather than an equal.

Tommy had trouble regulating his emotions. He had stormed out of Rye's classroom just weeks before when she asked him to write down what she was writing on the board. "You always pick on me. You always single me out and no one else. I won't stand for it anymore!" he declared as he ran to tell the psychologist what a horrible person she was. There were only three students in Tommy's math class, so if someone wasn't writing down her notes, she would make sure to call on them. They all worked at the same pace and had great understanding of each other. Tommy needed prompting to do most anything, so she did likely call his name more than the others, but not in a way that signaled annoyance with him, as she knew he couldn't help it.

The whole team had worked to prepare a new plan for Tommy that would reflect his needs, but his mother wanted him to be like everyone else. What parent didn't want their child to be "normal," whatever that really meant anymore? Rye understood that. She considered herself blessed that her daughters, six and eight, had met all of their milestones on time, and by all standards would have every opportunity available to them. She didn't have to think about things like if they'd be able to tie their shoes in middle school, or dress themselves, or make at least one friend.

Rye had been nominated for Teacher of the Year twice in her district, and one year she won. She had been known for being able to break down these walls with parents and build trust. Even if she started the year speaking to advocates instead of the parents, by the end of the year those advocates were often fired because the parents knew she had their child's best interest at heart. Even Tommy's mother had a positive relationship with Rye, but after years of coming to meetings with lawyers, she wasn't ready to stop yet. However, after the meeting, she did call to apologize to Rye for having to go through what she did at the meeting. It was why Rye generally didn't get angry at the parents for anything they did that they believed was advocating for their child. She and her mother had advocated for Don, but it got them nowhere. Where was someone to prove to her that the system wasn't broken?

Winnie

The smell of fish and curry filled the two-story townhouse Winnie shared with Don. It wasn't that she disliked curry or fish, but she hadn't cooked it, so it felt like an invasion of her personal space. It was only okay for her house to smell that way if she was the one who cooked it. Her pots and pans would be put back in a different location than where she had originally placed them. The spices would be placed on the rack in a different order after their use. While it was nice that Gordina was cleaning up after herself, Winnie liked everything a certain way. However, it was part of the bargain if she decided to bring Don home.

Don had been living in Willows, a psychiatric facility, for the past year, and to call it a nightmare would be an understatement. Every time Winnie walked into the piss-smelling building her stomach churned as she walked past the rooms. The doors were always left open, so she could see the man sitting in his boxers, tissues all over the room, staring blankly at the television. She could see the woman moaning in her bed, alone and always pained. She would check in with the nurses if Don had gone to any of the programs. He hadn't. Never sure when he last ate, she would check with the nurses if he'd gone to meals, and they would look at her as if she had asked them what he liked to eat when he was five years old. According to Don, he couldn't eat any of the food, and he couldn't drink anything because then he'd have to pee. Most of the time, he would be lying in bed in the same position he had been in the last time she saw him. His eyes were closed, but she knew he wasn't always sleeping, just wishing his life would come to an end.

Now, looking into the bedroom they used to share together, Don was lying in his bed just like he had at Willows. She forced him to go for a walk each day which was really more for her than it was for him. He wasn't doing anything to intentionally bother her, but the energy of depression seeped into the household and infected her. Just watching him lay there made her agitated. A bed was made next to him for Gordina, his around-the-clock care person she had hired in order to take Don home. Why she was paying someone to watch him lay in a bed she wasn't sure, but her memories were enough to keep Gordina there. She knew what Don was capable of, even if right now all he was doing was lying in a bed.

Just two years before, Don had been a newly retired, energetic man. He enjoyed taking out his kayak on the sound, visiting the beaches regularly breathing in the salty air. Winnie had convinced him to go to the beach with her once since coming home, desperate for anything that would give him an ounce of pleasure. Instead, he said it made him feel worse as he could no longer take out his kayak like he used to. Why he couldn't do this, Winnie could not comprehend. He was still a living, breathing, mobile human being, but he said he just could not do it, and they had to leave only minutes after being there. Don had been the most athletic person she ever knew, playing tennis with the neighbors, riding his bike, and running miles on a daily basis. He looked forward to dinners with Rye and her children, Emilie and Carter, playing catch with them both in the yard. This man had completely vanished in the blink of an eye and was now lying in bed while his caregiver took over Winnie's kitchen, filling the house with unfamiliar smells and making her feel like her home was no longer hers.

When Don did come out to talk to her, it was almost always about his bodily functions, unless he was also telling her about the fact that he was going to be arrested for a crime she knew he didn't commit. "I can't poop. I can't pee. It's a crisis" is all he would tell her. It was true that Don had prostate cancer. In the beginning of his downfall, this was one diagnosis that was clear and straightforward. It took months to convince him to remove his prostate, so worried was he that he would be impotent and unable to urinate on his own ever again. She wasn't sure why his impotence mattered, as they hadn't been intimate since long before he received the diagnosis. However, at this point, she had difficulty believing his concerns. His prostate had been removed with a full recovery. He could pee on his own even though he was still regularly refusing to drink. That was part of why Gordina was there because his blood pressure was so low due to dehydration. He wouldn't listen to Winnie, but he was too much of a people pleaser to deny Gordina. Winnie knew he was pooping too. He was on so many medications to make sure that he did, and she would smell the house, his bathroom leading right into the living room.

What Don wanted was to be sent to the Emergency Room. For all the hatred Winnie had for the healthcare system, the whole family agreed that Don liked it best when he was in the hospital. This was where he felt the most comfortable. It was where he'd spent much of his career. He liked being cared for by medical doctors and nurses. Winnie believed he wasn't doing this consciously and also knew enough to take what he told her with a grain of salt. She knew that he was not rational, and that he was not a reliable reporter of what was going on in his mind or his body. However, she also always had a hint of skepticism at her own judgment and worried that she was ignoring something serious. That had happened before too.

Winnie had moved herself upstairs, and this is where she stayed unless she was outside of the house. She was outside of the house a lot. She joined multiple groups to keep her occupied and to help her find support outside the home. Winnie was not one to sit and mope. She joined a caregiver's group and a spiritual group, volunteered at the food bank, and joined her neighbors for drinks, dinners, and trips to the theater. This was also why she hired Gordina. She needed to be able to leave the house without fear of what she would find when she returned.

Winnie was an avid exerciser herself, spending every morning at the gym and every afternoon out walking. The weather was finally starting to change, and she could feel Spring trying to come back after a winter that was dry, yet freezing. It was too cold to be at the beach, so she wandered around her neighborhood happy to be free of her visits to Willows and glad that her husband was safe at home. He was sleeping in a clean bed, and at least he was groomed and fed for the first time in a year.

The decision had not been easy. She knew that Don couldn't stay in Willows. She couldn't keep him there another minute. The social worker continued to tell her that he was improving, that they were starting to reach him. The psychiatrist on staff said he was the most difficult patient they had, and that his depression was "untreatable." The nurses tried their best, but Winnie knew it was not the most desired job, and most were trained solely to provide medication when needed. The program director continued to tell Winnie all of the programs that were available to Don, not listening to her frustration that they didn't make a difference because he wouldn't attend.

The problem with Winnie was she couldn't control her temper or her mouth. She would get so worked up with the people who worked there, that by now, she and the rest of the family were sure that they thought she was just as mentally ill as Don. She would snap at the social worker until the social worker had to leave the room and end the conversation. She would hang up on the psychiatrist angry that he couldn't give a better prognosis. Mostly, she confronted the program director, who had promised her a working program that wasn't working. She was spending their hard-earned money on this facility, and no one could help her. When Don was dehydrated, it was Winnie they called to deliver some Gatorade. They couldn't find him some juice? When a medication was needed and they ran out, Winnie had to drop everything and deliver it. She was entrusting these people to care for and cure her husband, and the situation just seemed to become more hopeless. What was worse, was that they no longer listened to her.

When Don would meet with them he would tell them that he was in jeopardy of going to jail, he had done something horribly wrong, and the police were out to get him. He told them that Winnie was seeing other men and trying to divorce him. While she did discuss divorce with a lawyer and her financial advisor to try and figure out what made the most sense for the family, none of this was actually true. However, the people who worked at Willows believed Don. They thought Winnie was cruel and didn't care for her husband, or at least that was how they treated her.

Winnie was aware of this and scheduled phone conferences with all of her children to help the people working there see who Don really was. They didn't believe that just two years ago, he had been an active man and that he had been a genius and successful endocrinologist who received so many letters and Thank You cards when he retired that Winnie had to find a large gift bag to store them all, as they didn't fit in the shoebox she had prepared. He was a walking encyclopedia of medical knowledge who had gone to Harvard when he was only sixteen after skipping the third grade. They didn't know how much he had deteriorated. He no longer wanted to watch sports on television, he couldn't read anything, he could barely walk around the facility as his muscles had atrophied so much from lying in bed, and he was regularly too dehydrated to stand up for long periods of time. Her children would reiterate what Winnie tried to convey meeting after meeting. The social worker would continue with empty promises to her children that they, at first, believed. The psychiatrist would share the same devastating diagnosis, and the program director would woo them as she had first charmed Winnie when she convinced her Willows was the best program for Don. She didn't know what to do, but she knew that Don couldn't stay there.

The biggest concern everyone had was Don's safety when he came home. He had ended up in Willows for a reason, and no one knew if he was safe at home. Winnie decided that she would hire a caregiver to live in the house at all times. This way she didn't have to worry about his safety, and he could be somewhere that he was clean, fed, and cared for. She would be able to find him the same services in an outpatient setting since he wasn't making use of the program anyway. What Winnie didn't realize was how difficult it would be for her to have a stranger living in her house.

Winnie was independent. She liked everything done her own way, and for the past year she had been living alone. While there was an emptiness in the house being by herself, all of her belongings were hers. She could watch what she wanted on television, and now Gordina watched her shows downstairs in the living room. The fridge was filled with unfamiliar foods she had to buy at the grocery store, and she couldn't cook in peace watching the news while she ate her dinner anymore. She had to make conversation with Gordina, who was absolutely lovely, but sometimes Winnie just didn't have the energy.

The timing of Don coming home was very purposeful on Winnie's part. She knew that Annie would need her after Avery was born in January and she had great concerns for Annie's wellbeing. Her pregnancy had been a nightmare. She had been sick the entire nine months, throwing up from start to finish. In the first trimester, she had lost fifteen pounds and been placed on Zofran that melted on her tongue because she couldn't even keep down water and a pill. Winnie was concerned that something wasn't right with the baby. She, of course, heard of women who were extremely sick during pregnancy, but something didn't seem right. Winnie also remembered what happened to Annie after she stopped breastfeeding Nicholas. She knew that Annie was prone to anxiety and depression and wanted to make sure she was available during the first six weeks of the baby's life.

While Winnie was taking her afternoon walk, she tried to forget about what was going on in her home, how much her life had changed in just a week, that she now had a permanent house guest and had banished herself to only the top floor of her home. Her phone rang and she saw it was Annie calling. She had been to visit Annie about two weeks before, knowing that it would be the last time in a while she'd be able to visit the baby as she didn't yet feel comfortable leaving Gordina and Don overnight in her house. When she left, all was well. Nicholas was in daycare and excited to have a new baby sister. Avery was the easiest baby she'd ever met, even though all she could compare her to were her own children and grandchildren, and Annie was happy. In fact, Winnie had been so relieved that after such a horrific pregnancy, there was a beautiful, healthy baby. Annie had been getting back into exercising, taking the baby for walks, and seemed to be enjoying herself on maternity leave much more than with Nicholas.

"Hello!" Winnie answered cheerfully. "How's my little Avery?"

Annie's voice was shaky. "She's fine, Mom."

"What's wrong?" Winnie's throat dropped into her stomach. She had received these calls before from Annie.

"Mom, I'm not okay."

"What do you mean you're not okay?" Annie burst into tears, and not just a hard sob, but hyperventilating as she cried her heart out. "I mean I'm not okay, Mom. I can't eat, I can't sleep, and I know what it is, but I don't know what to do about it. I'm already on medication. It's not working. I don't know what to do."

"Take a deep breath, Annie. You will get through this. You're going to call your doctor. You're not going to wait. You're going to tell them that the medication is not working, that you've been through this before, that this is hormonal, and you need help now," Winnie started to get into her defensive mode. There was something about the healthcare system that made her blood boil. She remembered how they hadn't helped her daughter last time, and she had been horrified at how the system had handled her husband over the past two years. She wasn't going to let that happen to Annie. "Where's Avery?" she panicked remembering that her daughter was home alone with the baby and was in the midst of a panic attack.

"She's asleep, Mom. She's fine. It's me. I'm the problem. She's perfect"

"You can't be so hard on yourself, Annie. You just can't. You're doing the best you can. You're going to take some deep breaths, and you're going to be okay. This too shall pass. You are going to get help." She stayed on the phone with Annie as she slowly began to come back to her breathing. Winnie stayed on the phone for her entire walk until she heard the baby crying in the background.

"I have to go feed Annie, Mom. I'll talk to you later."

She had taken Don home so she no longer had to be stuck going to Willows, but now she was trapped. Her daughter needed her, but she couldn't leave. She felt responsible for everyone's safety, but what could she do? She had to stay with Don. Winnie was no longer enjoying her walk.

Annie

The cat had been let out of the bag over the weekend. The morning had started the same way: vomiting, trembling, and feeling frozen in her bed. Michael had asked her if she was okay, and she lied and said that she was. On the weekends he wasn't so distracted by work and didn't need to drag a screaming Nicholas to preschool. "I'm just not feeling all that well," she lied. "I'll be okay."

It was a beautiful spring day, so they had decided to go for a walk on the bike path. She didn't really feel up for a walk, but she got herself dressed and outside. Even though it had been four days, her breasts were still full and painful. She had squeezed the tiniest bit of milk into the sink just to relieve the pressure. The hours she had spent on message boards didn't pay off, just like they hadn't the first time around. What was wrong with her body? Everyone else said they weaned over time and their milk dried up, or they decided to go cold turkey, put on two sports bras, took some ibuprofen, and within a couple of days the milk was gone. This wasn't how it worked for Annie. She had difficulty making enough milk when she needed it, and then when she tried to stop, her breasts decided it was the time to make milk. This was how she had gotten mastitis after Nicholas. She was walking around with cold cabbage leaves in her bra, a trick she had learned about from her doctor last time. While they helped slightly, she still worried she was getting an infection again.

They headed to the bike path with Avery in the stroller and Nicholas walking along picking up the biggest sticks he could find. For a moment, she felt normal if she could ignore the pain under her jacket. She could deal with painful breasts, but she couldn't handle the agitation that took over her body all day long. However, on the walk, it was like the bugs had left her body and joined the natural world around her instead. She even felt herself smile as they stopped next to a small creek, so Nicholas could practice trying to make rocks skip with Michael.

"Why don't we go to the diner for lunch," she suggested, having actually worked up an appetite for the first time in days. Maybe this was going to pass faster than she had previously believed.

"Are you sure you're up for it?" Michael asked, having just seen her throw up hours before in their bathroom.

"Yes, I could really go for some diner food."

Once Nicholas began whining he was hungry, they turned around and headed back to the car, so they could go to the diner. When she got into the diner out of the fresh air, the pain of her breasts became more than she could bear. She ran to the bathroom, unzipped her jacket, lifted her shirt, and squeezed her breasts into the toilet until she could breathe again. *Only enough to relieve the pressure*, she kept reminding herself, even though it was such a relief she wanted to empty her entire chest into the toilet.

When she returned to the table, the nauseous feeling began to creep into her throat again. She decided to just order soup and grilled cheese, still more than she had eaten in days, but Michael didn't know that. "That's all you're having?" he asked, used to her ordering a giant breakfast. When the food arrived, Annie could barely get the grilled cheese down and ended up sharing the rest with Nicholas who had already finished an entire sandwich himself.

Annie was exhausted. Both of the kids were napping, so she told Michael she was going to lay down and take a nap. She laid on the top of her bed like she used to every afternoon with Avery just days before. They would both sleep the afternoon away, and Avery would sleep so long that she would even get to squeeze in a shower when she woke. If Avery didn't sleep so well at night she would worry, but she had always heard the sleep begets sleep, and it sure was true with Avery. Sometimes, Avery would be awake in the bassinet when she came out of the shower just peacefully looking around waiting for her mommy. She tried to remember these times as she lay down on the bed. This time she didn't even have to worry about a baby or being woken. Michael would get them, and she could sleep as long as she needed.

She closed her eyes and took deep breaths just trying to let her body relax. Her breasts had been relieved and she hugged a pillow so she could lay on her side comfortably. She lay there for over a half an hour, but no sleep came. She began to feel the bugs back under her skin. Her body was restless, moving around trying to find a comfortable position so the bugs would stop moving and leave her alone. She could feel her breathing quicken, and her heart began racing even though her body was perfectly still. The sun shining through the windows made her feel like she shouldn't be lying in a bed. She decided she would just get up because lying down seemed to be making her worse. She remembered how much better she had felt on the walking trail, and she headed downstairs to watch television with Michael.

When she walked down the stairs, Michael looked up at her, and before giving him a chance to speak, the words that came out of her mouth were, "I'm not okay." Seconds later, she was having a full-blown panic attack. Her body was shaking as if she had just been rescued from the Titanic, shivering uncontrollably. She couldn't catch her breath as she just kept breathing in without exhaling. Michael held her firmly trying to get her to calm down, but she couldn't.

"What's going on? What's wrong?" Michael looked at her, worried.

Michael held Annie on the couch as she repeated the mantra, "I'm not okay. I'm not okay."

Michael had lived through postpartum depression with Annie before, and they had agreed that they would do whatever they needed to do to not let it happen again. The family couldn't afford it, not with another child in the mix. Michael held her as she sobbed and encouraged her to slow down her breaths. He sounded confident and reassuring, but Annie knew that this was making him nervous as well.

Michael wasn't used to seeing Annie this way. She usually had it all together. She was organized, energetic, and generally just wanted everyone around her to be happy. Aside from once a month, she rarely complained about anything. She was who he counted on to make plans and make sure the family had a social life. She loved organizing gatherings at the house and being with people. Even with all that she had been through with her dad over the past couple of years, it was rare that he saw her cry, and in those few instances that she did, her cries were warranted.

"Let's call the doctor," he suggested. After all, it was the gynecologist who had prescribed her Paxil in the first place. Clearly, it wasn't working.

"And what am I supposed to say?" she asked.

"Tell them what's going on."

Annie picked up the phone and dialed her gynecologist's office. It said if it wasn't a true emergency she would be charged a fee, so she hung up the phone. She wasn't dying. This wasn't an emergency.

"Why did you hang up?" Michael asked.

"They said I could be charged if it wasn't an emergency."

"So? Annie, this is an emergency. If you don't call back, I will."

Annie redialed the phone and waited to get the operator. She told the operator that she was experiencing panic attacks after weaning from breastfeeding, was already medicated, and needed to speak to a doctor. Within minutes, her call was returned.

She recognized the doctor on the other line immediately. She had only seen her one time at the practice. The doctor had taken a paper towel off the wall to show her the difference between ripping naturally and getting an episiotomy. Why she felt the need to scar her in this way before giving birth for the first time she wasn't sure. As the doctor ripped the paper towel to show how much less she would tear if she wasn't cut first, her expression remained blank and lifeless. Maybe she had delivered too many babies, maybe she had dealt with too many difficult mothers, but this was not who Annie wanted delivering her baby. In her practice, mothers visited all of the doctors in the practice before giving birth because their baby would be delivered by whoever happened to be on call that day. Luckily, neither time was this woman.

She explained what she was experiencing to the doctor on the phone. As she began explaining, her panic attack worsened. Through shortened breaths and flowing tears, she told the doctor that she was experiencing postpartum depression much more severely than she ever had before. She explained that she couldn't sleep, she couldn't eat, she was vomiting, and she couldn't stand the feeling in her body.

"This is not normal. You need to contact your psychiatrist immediately," the doctor said in a monotone voice.

If it wasn't normal, then why did they screen her so many times for these symptoms? Every time she went to their office, every check-up she brought her babies to at the pediatrician's office after giving birth, she was given a survey to see if she was experiencing signs of postpartum depression. While it wasn't a desired experience, it must be somewhat normal if all women were screened for it so frequently. "I don't have a psychiatrist," she choked out through sobs.

"Then who is prescribing you Paxil?"

"You guys are."

"Well, it clearly isn't working." *No shit, Sherlock.* "You need to contact a psychiatrist immediately." Well, so much for that help because it was Sunday afternoon.

She didn't want to call Winnie, but she knew that was who would be able to calm her down. It wasn't that Michael wasn't trying, but Winnie just had a way; she always had. It was the afternoon, so Annie guessed that Winnie was probably out on a walk. She knew that it was going to cause her anxiety to let her know what was going on, but she made the call anyway.

In fact, who she really wanted to talk to was Don. If anyone understood anxiety and depression, it was him. He was the one who helped her get on Paxil in the first place when her symptoms of anxiety began when she was much younger. Her father had reassured her that she would feel better, he had no doubts. There was something about his confidence in her recovery that made her feel confident too. She had been in her early twenties just starting in the workforce. She had become debilitated by perfectionism and was unable to function at the thought of going to work each day. Her doctor had prescribed other medications that didn't work, and her father finally told her to ask for Paxil. It had been a miracle for her, that and the incredible therapist she had found to help her work through her issues of self-acceptance and realistic expectations.

Unfortunately, she hadn't had a conversation with her father since their last family vacation.

They were hiking in the Adirondack Mountains. Although he was hiking with the family, he had seemed distant. He had arrived at the vacation with bruises surrounding both of his eyes. It looked like he had gotten into a bar room brawl, and he looked like a raccoon. It was hard to see the bruises on Don, a man who stood over six feet tall and could always be counted on to lift the heavy items when it was time to move or carry in your bags when you came to visit. Winnie hadn't told them what had happened in advance. This was how both her parents operated, which they claimed was to protect the girls, but what they didn't realize is that it made the girls more nervous that something would go wrong and they wouldn't know about it because neither parent would tell them.

Don had fallen down the stairs. Aunt Vicki had been visiting, and she wasn't an easy person for Don to be around. She didn't like him, and he knew it. She had never thought he was good enough for Winnie. He worked too much and didn't spend enough time with his family. He wasn't enough of a partner for Winnie, in her opinion.

When Don retired, he had cut back on his Ativan after much persuasion from his daughters, but on the day Vicki came to visit, he took a little extra. Don always enjoyed his wine or beer, but on this day he claimed he drank a little more than usual. He had stood up and fallen down a flight of wooden stairs, landing at the bottom right on his face. He immediately began to seize, and Winnie called the ambulance. When they arrived on the scene, he had stopped seizing, but was confused. They told him he needed to get in the ambulance and get checked out at the hospital, but he refused to go. Doctors tended to be the worst patients. Her father would never know what really caused the fall and what happened to his brain afterwards.

The next day on the trip, Don ended up in the hospital again. It was Cade's birthday while they were away, so like her parents, Rye and Annie had kept it a secret from her, letting her sleep in. She didn't have children, so they figured she may as well enjoy a good night of sleep on her birthday. In the middle of the night, Don had awoken to extreme pain and a high fever, and was peeing blood. Winnie and Don had rushed to the nearest emergency room, but were back by breakfast with a dose of antibiotics for Don. While Don went to rest, Annie and Rye told Cade what had happened to their father. It was the beginning of the urinary problems that would be diagnosed as prostate cancer. It was the beginning of the end of her father as she knew him, and boy did she miss him right now.

Rye

Rye stood over the copier copying page after page of data. She had already gone through her emails, printing off every email correspondence she had ever had with regard to Lee. This meant that every time she modified her work she had to print this and give it to the parents. Every worksheet Lee had ever completed needed to be copied. She had to copy the phone log of every time she had spoken to Lee's parents on the phone. She knew she was going to be at the copier for hours, so she texted Will to let him know she would be home late. Whenever she had a request for records, she liked to get it all done at once. Otherwise, it was too disruptive to her school day because it took hours. Her boss would let her know with only two to three days' notice, so Rye would pick a night she knew they were eating leftovers for dinner and would stay after school to print and copy her paperwork.

She hadn't been told why this request for records was taking place. Oftentimes, parents did this just for some information for an outside provider they had hired without realizing how much work went into it for Rye. They really just wanted their child's report card and special education paperwork, but didn't know to ask for just that, so they asked for a whole record. When that happened, it meant that Rye had to copy everything.

Parents tended to apologize later when they received the giant folder of every piece of paper their child had ever written their name on, but by then, Rye had already lost an afternoon with her children. As she stood there mindlessly copying her data binder, her mind drifted to the school year before.

She was standing in the library copying her phone log, and her mind was anything but empty. It was the first time she had ever felt she couldn't reach a student and believed he belonged in a different environment. Victor was in seventh grade, and he was fourteen years old. He was smearing feces on the wall and was selectively mute. On every standardized test, he performed at or above grade-level; as he was a very smart student, but he couldn't produce any work. There was a history of abuse in the home, but nothing had been proven, even though child protective services had been called on multiple occasions. His father was an alcoholic and his mother was mentally ill, so support at home was limited.

Rye had tried to warn the parents that an outplacement would be her recommendation over the phone. She repeatedly notified them of the lack of progress Victor was making at school. Sadly, his seventh-grade year was going so much better than the year before, that if she didn't advocate, he was going to go through to another school year with the same behavior. In sixth grade, Victor wouldn't even step foot in a classroom. He stood at his locker all day long, staring into space. He refused to speak to anyone for entire days, so based on that, he had made strides. However, given his intellect, his functioning was dismal compared to a typical seventh grader.

Victor had begun talking in class, but never on topic. Now, after a question had been asked to the class, Victor would raise his hand. "Mrs. Hue?" he would ask, "Should I have popcorn chicken for lunch?"

He would come close to Rye's desk after class, smelling strongly of feces and body odor, and point out a typo she had made on her class handout. He would ask if he could have items from his desk because he wanted to store them in his locker. Victor obsessively asked Rye about the schedule, especially if there were changes, but even when it was the same as it was every week. He would stand at the front of her room where it was posted just staring at it.

When he was put with a group, Victor turned his chair the other way or hid in the bathroom. At least he was stepping foot into a classroom, but he wasn't participating or interacting with any other students. He was given an aide, but it was fruitless because she couldn't get him to complete any work. The only time he did anything was sitting alone with Rye. Only then would he type one sentence which would take him half of a period, concerned that his sentence wasn't good enough and getting distracted by random questions he could look up on the internet. It was better than staring at a locker, but he wasn't okay.

The psychologist tried to get him outside help because he was only on medication for ADHD which he took at night causing sleepless nights. He regularly fell asleep during class, and admitted that he immediately took a nap everyday as soon as he got home. His mother claimed they didn't have money to pay for additional help, and anyone the psychologist recommended was dismissed as not competent. Victor's mother told continuous lies of all that he did outside of school that Rye knew weren't true, especially the yearbook club, which took place in her room. He spent the whole time sitting by himself in a corner looking over old yearbooks while his mother described him as being an "integral" member of the club. Since the only members of the club were him, his sister, and his sister's best friend, his attendance alone made him somewhat essential. However, he was really just obsessing over any mistakes he could find in the old year books. Victor spent most of his day obsessing and hoarding materials. He wanted to keep highlighters, paperclips, post-it notes, dry erase markers, anything the class was using, even though he would refuse to use them for anything productive. Victor just wanted to keep it all in his locker.

He was going to be fifteen years old, and needed therapeutic intervention. His whole day needed to be this way. He needed to be in a situation where he was held accountable all day rather than switching rooms with his main education coming from a paraprofessional. When it came time to make this recommendation at his end of year meeting, Rye swallowed hard and told the parents, "I am recommending outplacement."

His mother began screaming at her. "I am not sending my child to another school! He's staying at this one! If you don't keep him here, then I am going to pull him out! If you don't keep him here, I am going to come back with more people, and you just wait!" She kept leaving the room and coming back over and over again. Each time she walked back in she made another threat at Rye.

Rye wasn't surprised when days later, they received a letter that the parents were taking the district to court. She knew what this entailed, but she felt the recommendation she made was necessary for Victor. She knew how much time was going to be wasted with the district lawyer and going through all of her paperwork, but she wasn't willing to back down. The team supported her fully and felt that the decision was the right one to be making.

It was February, the day before break, and on top of having to put together all of Victor's records, Rye had to attend a ridiculous professional development course in Hartford, Connecticut. It was all about the new standardized test being given out to students and how to prepare students to do well on it. She had called her mother on the way there since it was about an hour drive, and she knew her mother was home with her father. He had just come home from one of the most prestigious mental hospitals in the country. They had put him through two different rounds of electroshock therapy, rearranged his medication, and claimed that he was ready to go home while simply attending an outpatient program daily.

That day, as she was talking to her mom, Winnie had excitement in her voice. "He got up even before I did today," she said, "and drove himself this time."

"Mom, is he supposed to be driving?"

"The doctor said it was fine and that it was a good sign if he wanted to drive."

"Are you sure he went to the program?"

"He said he was going to the program." Rye felt the color drain from her face. Suddenly, she had to pay more attention to the road or she was going to drive right off of it. How could her mother be so stupid? She let her father drive himself to the program? Rye tried to let it go as she pulled into the state education building ready to lose hours of her life she would never be able to get back. She wouldn't have been enthralled by the presentation anyway, but now all she could think about was Don. Had her mother confirmed that he made it to the program? She was scared to ask.

Also, she couldn't stop thinking about Victor. Was she really ready to take the stand? She would have to get up in front of the parents and make statements about their child that would be hard to say to her worst enemy. She just wanted to be at school, planning out how she was going to organize her testimony, preparing to copy her records after school. She decided to text Will and tell him she would be home late. Even though she could wait until after break to make her copies, Rye wanted to get it over with. When the professional development course ended early, she drove the whole hour back from Hartford deciding she was going to get her paperwork done before break. She needed to distract herself from thoughts of her mother and father.

When she got back to the school, the day had ended and the students were gone. It was supposed to be an exciting time where teachers could finally forget about all that was going on at work for a week, but Rye just couldn't. She brought her binders and phone logs to the copier and began the process. Hours went by as she went through reams of paper, copying three quarters worth of work, data sheets, and phone calls. She logged on to a library computer and printed her mountain of emails. Since every assignment for every single class was modified for Victor, her email list was extensive, but she printed them all.

When she got in the car, she decided to call her mom again. There was a pit in her stomach when her mother didn't answer. Her mother always answered. Her father didn't go to the program, and he didn't come home. She knew it. She kept calling until her mother answered.

"I can't talk right now. The police are here."

"Mom, just tell me, did he go to the program?"

"No, he didn't."

Rye decided she was going straight to her mother's house. She only lived ten minutes away. She needed to find out for herself what her father had done. Why were the police there? Had he committed a crime when he was supposed to be at the program? She knew that he had become unstable over the past year, but he was a man who would have never hurt a fly. Did they find his body? It wouldn't be his first attempt over the past year to end his own life.

As Rye pulled into the driveway, she saw the police car parked on the street. The front door was open, so she walked right in. Her first instinct was to go hug her mother, but her mother didn't look like she wanted a hug. She was pacing back and forth, her body rigid, yet it looked like every part of her was moving.

"They found him," she said.

"What do you mean they found him? Where? Where did he go? Is he alive?"

"He's in Rhode Island." What the hell was her father doing in Rhode Island? "The police there are following him. His car has been tracked. It looks damaged and like it's been in water. The police are going to follow him back to the house, where it looks like he's going now."

They waited at the house together, neither of them speaking other than Winnie repeatedly saying, "I should have never let him take the car. I should have known."

Two hours later, her father's car pulled into the driveway. She wasn't sure how he had been able to drive the car anywhere. It looked almost totaled. It was dented in the front, on the sides, and had scratches covering it. Don stepped out of the vehicle, actual icicles hanging from his hair and his clothing. He had driven his vehicle into the water. He tried to kill himself, yet again, but it hadn't worked.

As her father looked at the police car that had followed him and then at the one sitting in the driveway, she saw his entire pant leg change color. He had pissed himself. Her sixty-eight- year-old father had just peed his pants in front of her. He was shivering as the police covered him with a blanket. "Am I going to jail?" he asked pathetically. It was like watching a five-year-old who didn't understand the way the world worked. He thought he was in trouble, that he had broken the law.

"No, you're going to the hospital," the policeman answered firmly but with sympathy in his eyes.

"Did I do something wrong?" The policeman didn't answer him. Most wouldn't consider lying to your wife, driving your car into a lake, and then driving around on the road in a state of mania the right thing to do, but her father wasn't going to prison.

Rye would later learn that it was the second time her father tried to kill himself that day. When he got to the hospital, he admitted that he tried to slash his wrists in the morning. He didn't want Winnie to see, so he quickly put on his jacket and told her that he was going to the program. He did, in fact, drive to the program, but when he got to the front door, he was so worried that someone was going to see his wrists, that he got back in the car and left. Not knowing what to do, he got on the highway and just drove. He drove until he saw signs for a lake and decided that was how he would end his life. Instead, he was back in the hospital, and now they had to figure out what to do with him next.

Don looked at Rye, ashamed for her to see him like this. "I did something stupid," was all he could say. "I did something really stupid."

Her mother went to the hospital with Don, but Rye had to get home to her kids. When she got home, Emilie and Carter were so excited for the start of break. Carter handed Rye her backpack full of the work she got to take home. It was heavy with the books she always carried around. Carter was always reading. Rye went to put down the bag to open it, and all of a sudden she got stuck there.

She had worn herself out to the point that she threw out her back putting down her daughter's backpack. She yelled to Will for help to get the kids away from her so she could quietly cry to herself after what she had just witnessed, but also to get herself out of the stuck position. She was bent over and couldn't lift her body. Fortunately, Will was a physical therapist. He came running upstairs from the basement where he was exercising when she texted him there was a problem with Don and Winnie. He helped her get herself positioned on the floor where she could lay on her stomach. He ushered the girls out of the room to go watch television while he prepared dinner. Tears streamed down Rye's face onto the carpet where she rested her head. That was how she spent most of her February break. It was also the final straw that led Don to a year in Willows.

Now, while she stood by the copier, Don was home again. He had just come home a week ago. He had some woman watching him whose name Rye could never remember, but she still didn't know if her mother had made the right decision. This time, there was no car. Her mother had gotten rid of the car while Don was at Willows. It would be awhile, if ever, before she trusted him behind the wheel again, and in his current state, he wasn't trying to drive anyway.

Thankfully, Rye also wasn't preparing to go to court, as it had never been scheduled. Victor's parents decided to pull him out of special education in the end, so that the school couldn't outplace him. If he wasn't receiving services, then there couldn't be a recommendation made by the team that he receive them elsewhere. Already, this school year, Victor's parents reinstated his services, and after all of their fighting, agreed to outplace him. He had spent the beginning of eighth grade doing no work. He actually managed to have a zero in most of his classes meaning he didn't even attempt one piece of work in most of them. His parents had no choice.

No, this time was different. Her father was home, safe and sound. She was going to be home late, but she was going to go home and relax with her family. There was no family crisis, at least not yet.

Cade

"I hate God, I hate Jesus, I hate the president, but mostly I hate you," Morgan seethed. "And if I tell you any different I won't mean it. And if I tell you that I mean it, I still won't mean it." Then she walked over and flicked Cade in the leg.

Luckily, the rest of the class had left the room and she had called for the special education teacher to come on the prepaid cell phone that was given to her since there was no intercom or phones that connected the trailers. That way, she could at least get the other kids to their special. So much for a planning period on this day. She could tell that Morgan was getting ready for a meltdown as soon as she arrived that morning. She had climbed under her desk and was flicking pencil shavings, staples, and small bits of crayon at the other students in the class. Rye had to ignore her because she had a room of twenty-two first graders to teach, so she had continued on with the morning meeting and math centers, leaving Morgan to herself.

As soon as Cade returned from dropping the students at their special, the special education teacher excused herself, claiming she had something else to do. Rye was left in the room with Morgan yelling at her. Although she had to admit that she was a bit flattered to be held to the same pedestal God and Jesus, Cade had learned that with Morgan, it was best not to engage. It had taken her a few months to learn this, but that was the case with teaching.

It was just like with Redding, who all year kept pooping his pants. She tried hand signals, not having him bring extra clothes to school, a timer, anything to stop him from pooping his pants and sitting there while the stench filled the entire classroom as he kept it to himself until he made a mess in the bathroom trying to clean up. He didn't stop until she brought him outside one morning while the teaching assistant was there and told him that there was a new rule in school that he wasn't allowed to poop his pants. Redding was such a rule follower, that she figured it was worth a shot. She told him that if he continued to poop his pants, he wouldn't be allowed to go to second grade. It never happened again.

Now, Cade sat at her desk, trying to look busy on her computer not engaging with Morgan. Morgan was a product of fetal alcohol abuse and she was now a foster child living with a very loving, but not always warm, family. She was on significant medication for bipolar disorder and most of the time was very regulated. Cade didn't admit this to anyone else, but she was her personal favorite. She watched Morgan walk over to a plant Cade had brought to spruce up the classroom and pick at the leaves. She was trying anything to get Cade riled up.

Although she was beginning to feel the anger rising a bit inside, she didn't let Morgan see this.

Finally, with ten minutes to spare in her twenty minutes to herself she was supposed to have, Morgan came over and asked, "Can we play Pictionary?"

"Sure," Cade replied, and so they did until the other students returned, and that was the end of Morgan's tantrum. She had also learned it was best not to discuss it, or they could end up right back where they started. Morgan was desperate for attention and sometimes enjoyed negative attention even more than positive attention. Unfortunately for Cade, it took many trying situations to learn this.

The students came back, and it was immediately time for reading centers. Cade ran around the room setting these up as she talked to the students about each one. With first graders, the routine couldn't be changed, not even slightly. They noticed everything. One of the students pointed out, "Why aren't you sitting with the pointer showing us in our groups?" Cade patiently continued setting up and calmly began her centers, even though inside she was flustered.

This was what she just didn't have the energy for anymore. Every day was so damn hard. She had looked forward to the idea that every day on the job would be different when she got into teaching, but she wasn't prepared to have every day feel like she had completed an entire school year. She wasn't prepared for a meth addict mother to corner her in her trailer on her way home after school one day, telling her she better get rid of the teaching assistant. She wasn't prepared to buy jackets for two of her students who came every day without them. It was North Carolina, but the winter was still cold. She wasn't prepared to have a student dictate a reflection sheet for swearing only to be told by the parent signing the form that her expectations were too high. She definitely hadn't prepared to be isolated in a trailer with no one to provide her students with materials, counseling, a nurse, books, snacks, art, and music except her.

Cade had written a play that the students performed for the school, the students had made their own papier-mache globes, and she gave a child his inhaler every day for his asthma even though she had no idea how to know whether he was doing it correctly. Every month, Cade wrote a grant, and had finally been granted one that spring. It was a Target field trip grant for the students to go gem panning and create their own rock encyclopedias. They did a donation drive for the SPCA, bake sales that the students organized including handling the money, and she even had the animals brought into the school to help the students see who they were helping. Cade had created reading journals for every student in the class using the school book binder, one by one. The kids had grown plants, built a volcano, made their own slime all with materials she bought for the class. She had given it her all and she was burnt out. Even when she had a vacation, she spent her time thinking about school. She researched new ideas, and she perused the stores spending more of her money. There was no listening center at the school, so she recorded her own voice for the students to listen to while they read library books that she took out and exchanged every week.

On top of it all, she worried about her mother and father. She would never forget the call she got while she was still in graduate school in the fall. She knew that she was the last to be called because she was always the last to know. Being the youngest, her parents tried to protect her the most, but she was glad they told her. Her father was going to the hospital.

Cade had been a little naive about her father her whole life. Being the youngest, she had her older sisters to look out for her. No one really talked about her father's addiction. Rye would get the most upset at family occasions, and tell him he was taking too much medication. It was true that he would fall asleep in the middle of a conversation while the whole family was gathered around. She did remember driving home with her father after Annie's wedding as he kept falling asleep at the wheel, her mother screaming at him to let her drive. Don claimed that he had only drank decaf coffee that morning, and they just needed to pull over and get some regular coffee. He agreed to drink his coffee in the passenger seat, and Winnie went to go get him a cup. He sat down facing out of the car, and was immediately asleep with his feet out the door. Cade sat there in shock, leaving him in that position until her mother came out and picked his legs up into the car. He also forgot her birthday every year even though she was the only child left in the house, and would often tell her "Happy Birthday" days later when she had even celebrated at the house, but he had somehow failed to notice.

When she thought about her father, she thought about the man who came to her dance recitals and cheered like he was watching a game, watched her graduate from college, who always made her feel like she was beautiful and special. Her father loved fiercely, even though he spent most of his time working. His love was unconditional for all three of his girls. They could be who they wanted and what they wanted, even though they all ended up choosing the same career path. While he could be passive at times, he was kind and loyal. That being said, he was also absent in her everyday life. He'd never come to a parent-teacher conference, picked her up or dropped her off at dance class, made her dinner, or helped her with her homework. He had spent very little quality time with her growing up. However, she didn't know the addict that was hiding inside him, slowly causing him to deteriorate.

Her father was going to the hospital to detox. Rye was always giving him a hard time about his use of benzodiazepines. She knew that he took Ativan throughout the day and Klonopin to sleep at night, but she didn't know the extent to which he was taking these drugs. He was a doctor, and a good one at that. She trusted his judgment and knew that he functioned better than most people. He worked his tail off day after day, still finding the energy to exercise every day, but he never made it to his bed before he passed out on the couch. She had chalked it up to a hard day's work, but it was clearly more. Now, he was checking himself in, and ready to rid himself of the toxins he had been filling his body with for all these years, taking more and more to function at his job and as a father. Once he retired, he tried to take himself off of the drugs, or at least reduce their amount, but he couldn't, at least not without dire consequences.

Cade was burnt out and she wasn't sure which was the lead cause. She didn't know if she could continue doing what she was doing every day. While she wasn't abusing drugs, she was drinking herself to sleep each night in order to rid her mind of work. On the weekends, she almost never made it home, sleeping on her friends' couches because she was too drunk to drive home. She was young and having fun, right? She kept telling herself she would stop when Ryan moved out to North Carolina. However, as the year went on, this was seeming less likely. Ryan had become more distant. She could tell that he was sick of hearing about work, but that was all she ever wanted to talk about. He was still living the graduate school life, studying, but partying with their group of friends. Sometimes talking to him made her feel worse and ache for her old life. She had no other way to distract herself. She wasn't like her father—at least she didn't think so.

Winnie

Don was crawling around on all fours like a rabid dog. He had been taken over by another being. Her docile husband was manic, restless, and couldn't stop his body from moving. He couldn't stand up and walk normally. He just crawled around on the floor telling Winnie that he couldn't stand how he was feeling. There was something seriously wrong with him. He knew it. He didn't want to live anymore. There was no way he could go on with the feeling that he had. Winnie had no choice; she had to take him to the Emergency Room. She didn't know what else to do.

This was the tipping point, but Don hadn't been himself since the family trip to the Adirondacks. Since he had gotten the urinary infection and fell down the stairs, something had changed in Don. He seemed like he couldn't stand living in his own skin anymore. He made comments about not wanting to live anymore and knowing there was something deeply wrong with him. The only thing that calmed him down was Ativan, and he was taking more than ever before. The more he took, the more he kept needing it to take the edge off. Winnie was debating what to do with Don. She knew he needed help, but to what extent?

He had retired the summer before, and it was no easy retirement. He had been in a business relationship with a greedy, self-centered man who made it very difficult for Don to leave. In fact, it turned out that his partner was involved in illegal transactions with patients, so he didn't want Don to leave the practice because he didn't want this to come to light. If Don left the practice, it meant the practice would have to close down. Don never wanted to let anyone down, but he had been planning the retirement for over a year, with Winnie as his cheerleader to follow through with the plan.

For years he worked with the same man at a private endocrinology practice. They were an old-fashioned doctor's office where Don didn't just know his patients as patients, he knew them as people. He knew their families and went above and beyond in his care of them. Don had never used a computer to keep patient records. He wrote down notes and spoke into a recorder on his own time in order to keep track of their medical history. When he was with a patient, his focus was solely on them, not on typing into a computer and keeping a time slot. All of the girls had worked in his office over their summers at some point in their lives, and they couldn't believe that the office staff still used typewriters. Stepping into his office was like stepping back in time, which was part of what kept the patients coming, but seemed inefficient to Don's daughters. They couldn't fathom that they were spending their summers organizing folders in alphabetical order when their own doctors just went into a computer system and clicked on their names.

For the duration of their practice, there had been no equality. His partner made seventy percent of the profits to Don's thirty percent. His partner never worked on Fridays and Don never once took a day off, not even when he got into a major car accident on his way into work. He got the car to the office and didn't take care of the car or himself until after he had seen his last patient for the day. Don didn't care that it wasn't fair. He made enough money for his girls to go to college without loans, for the family to live in a modest house, and to meet all of their needs. Don would do anything to avoid confrontation, so when he finally retired, it was a big deal for him.

Winnie helped Don get a lawyer and get himself out of the practice unscathed. She collected all of the cards and letters people wrote to Don. She couldn't believe the way people were reacting to his retirement. It was as if they were losing a good friend, a relative, someone near and dear to them they had known a long portion of their lives. They thanked him for helping them and changing their lives forever. So many of us set out to make a difference in the lives of others through our work, and that is what Don had done. Winnie was nervous for his retirement because he had put his heart and soul into his work, and she wasn't sure what would be there when it was gone.

Don surprised her his first year of retirement. He was the lightest and happiest she had seen him since they met as camp counselors forty years before. Instead of burying himself in his work, he was doing the activities he enjoyed. He was spending time with Rye and his granddaughters and was finally willing to take trips to see Annie and Nicholas. In fact, Winnie felt connected to him in a way she hadn't since before they had children. She found herself in the shower thinking to herself how lucky she was for her life.

Now, as she stared at Don on the floor, crawling around like an animal, she watched her luck slip through her fingers. It was like her life had tripped over a rock, and her lucky coin fell into a sewer grate before she could catch it. She was supposed to be driving to Annie's house to watch Nicholas while she and Michael went to a wedding. Normally, she would have kept this a secret from the girls, taken Don to the hospital, resolved the situation, and then maybe she would tell them as an afterthought, but she couldn't this time.

Winnie decided she would start with Rye. She always started with Rye if there was something important to tell. Rye could handle anything. She was tougher than her other girls. She would give her advice on what to say to the others if she had any. "Hi honey," she said when Rye answered.

"Hi Mom," Rye said, sounding out of breath.

"Where are you right now?"

Rye knew that this meant her mother had bad news to tell her. While there were very few times her mother had to tell her something, if she did, she always wanted to know what Rye was doing first. She wanted to make sure Rye wasn't driving, that she wasn't with friends, that she was somewhere safe and alone to be told news that would change her life forever. "What is it, Mom?"

"Your father needs to go to the hospital. He's been abusing Ativan, as you know, and it's gotten to the point where he needs medical help to get off of it."

"Okay, is he okay right now? Is he safe?

"He's very agitated right now, and he's not doing well. We need to go now, but I needed you to know because we may be there for a while. It may take days, and then we need to figure out our next steps."

"What can I do?"

"Nothing, honey. I want you to enjoy your day with whatever you had planned with the girls."

"I love you both. Please keep me posted, Mom."

Winnie then moved on to Annie and Cade telling them the same story. She was thankful that Annie was so understanding about her not being able to watch Nicholas for the wedding. She didn't know why she had been so nervous to tell Annie she couldn't do it. She didn't want to let her down, but at the end of the conversation, Annie didn't sound much like she wanted to be heading to a wedding anyway. Annie was the most fragile of her daughters as it was.

She tried not to think too much about Don's stay at the hospital as he detoxed. Don writhed with discomfort in the hospital bed; his words didn't make sense, and his thoughts were not rational. The doctors had taken him off of Ativan so quickly, he had gone into acute withdrawal. They put him on new medication that caused him to have a psychotic episode. He just kept telling her that he wanted to die, that he couldn't live this way. Winnie watched him feeling completely helpless. She also felt panicked because she had to figure out where Don was going to go next. He wasn't just going to stay in the hospital.

No one listened to her. She felt like she was screaming in the middle of an airport and all of the people just continued to hustle and bustle around her trying to get to their flights ignoring the sound. No one believed her that this wasn't what her husband had been like his whole life. He had gone from letters of admiration and gratitude to being treated like an addict from the streets. Winnie kept correcting the doctors as they spoke to him that he was Dr. Sanders and not Mr. Sanders. She wanted them to know who their patient was. Don had always put so much care into knowing his patients and their families, and no one in the hospital seemed to care to know his history. They knew that he was there because he was abusing a drug, and that seemed to be all they needed to know. She kept asking what was going to happen next, but no one would give her a straight answer or help her find the right placement for Don.

There was no sense in thinking about it now because nothing had helped Don. There Winnie was watching Gordina knit while she watched a sitcom on television. Winnie found sitcoms to be obnoxious. She thought to herself that if this continued, she would need to purchase a television for the bedroom upstairs. Don was lying in bed in the same position he stayed in all day. He wasn't crawling around her living room floor anymore, but he wasn't living a life of any quality either.

Winnie didn't only have Gordina coming into her house, but a nurse and an occupational therapist too. She tried not to remember why they were there because it had been so traumatizing what Don did to himself and, ultimately, his family. It was time for her afternoon walk, and she was going to take that time to unwind. It wasn't like there was anything she had to do in her house, but Winnie was very affected by the energy of others. All of the commotion of the people in her house felt like an invasion of her space. She felt like her life was no longer hers.

She stepped out into the fresh air feeling as though she had just been released from prison. It wasn't the most beautiful day out, overcast and cloudy, but Winnie was glad she had the freedom to leave her house. She walked the same route every day. In fact, some days she had been getting so irate in her house that she had started running. Just as she was beginning to start to jog, she heard the phone ring. It was Michael, Annie's husband, calling.

Annie

The vomiting was violent. Michael held a garbage can up to the bed for Annie, but all that was coming out was clear water and yellow bile. It was uncontrollable. Avery slept peacefully through it all as Annie puked just inches away from her head. She was shaking uncontrollably, and she couldn't get out of bed. The retching noises had traveled down the stairs as he rushed up to see what was going on. He had seen Annie struggling over the past couple of weeks, throwing up here and there. It had been a bit like her pregnancy where she would run to the bathroom, but then come back and be able to function. She hadn't been eating normally, but Michael knew it would take a while after starting hormone therapy for Annie's body to regulate.

Michael had seen Annie cry before, but not like this. Annie couldn't breathe, she was sobbing so hard. Michael didn't even know if he was going to be able to leave long enough to get Nicholas to daycare. He didn't know if Annie could be alone with Avery. Even though Annie had experienced postpartum depression with Nicholas, he never worried for her safety or Nicholas's. She didn't feel good, and wasn't herself for a while, but he never worried that she would neglect or harm Nicholas, or herself for that matter. This time, he wasn't so sure.

She looked haggard. She hadn't dried her hair the night before, so her frizzy, brown, curls were hanging over her face and sticking out on the sides. Her slim frame was hunched over unable to straighten up. Michael had to hoist her body over his arm and assist her down to the couch in the living room. He set her up with another garbage can because she wasn't capable of running to the bathroom. Annie vomited the whole way. It was a blessing Nicholas was such a good sleeper as they rushed past his room.

Michael and Annie had both been hopeful that Annie would improve. She had gone to the doctor after her panic attack. They had gotten her into the office that Monday morning. It turned out if you told a doctor's office that you were experiencing postpartum depression, they moved much faster to help you. Annie had met with the doctor.

"I'm not doing well," she had told the doctor who had delivered both of her children. Through tears she added, "I don't want to lose months of Avery's life like I did with Nicholas. It's like it was with him only amplified. I'm so much worse."

"Well, luckily, this time we know what it is, and we know that postpartum depression is largely hormonal. First, we can increase your Paxil. It may be that during this time period, you need more than you did before.

Your baseline this time may be different than what it was the other times in your life when you took it. It also sounds like your body is low on estrogen. Aside from other hormone changes that take place, that is a hormone that takes time to return to normal after having a baby. We can speed that along by using hormone therapy." She pulled a sample in a tube out of her desk. "This is cream you can use that should start working immediately, but don't use it more than once per day. I'm also going to prescribe you an estrogen patch that you can start using, but it will take a few days to begin working. This cream should make up for the lapse in time."

"Do you really think this will help?"

"There is no way of knowing for sure, but there has been success for many women using hormone therapy to relieve symptoms of postpartum depression. I do recommend that you also go speak to someone. I'll give you the information of some therapists I know who are known for their work in the postpartum period."

Annie left feeling hopeful. She put the cream on immediately in the car. Within hours, she was feeling better. She actually had an appetite for the first time in weeks and made herself a sandwich. Michael had taken the day off of work that day, so Annie could go see as many doctors as she needed. She also had made a visit with her primary care doctor that afternoon in case the gynecologist wasn't helpful. Although, this time, they had listened to her, unlike when she went after Nicholas.

At her primary care office, she told the doctor what was going on. The doctor offered to prescribe her Ativan to help take the edge off, but suggested she see a psychiatrist because it didn't seem like having her gynecologist managing her psychiatric medication was the best idea. Annie really wanted some help to sleep, but she would never take Ativan, not after what it did to her father. The doctor prescribed her ten Xanax and then recommended she see a psychiatrist. "You don't have to take any, but if you really can't sleep, at least you have something until you can get an appointment with a psychiatrist." She gave Annie the information for who she usually referred patients to. "He's not the most responsive, but that's who we refer to."

Annie wasn't sure how that was helpful, but she decided she would find a psychiatrist and make an appointment as soon as she could. She took the Xanax prescription home and decided that if she really couldn't sleep, she would take some. She picked up her estrogen patch and the Xanax at the pharmacy and went home feeling lighter than she had in weeks. She was going to get better. She had support and medications that would help her.

Mornings were still difficult for Annie over the next couple of days, but she wasn't throwing up, and she could get out of bed. She and Michael decided that she would get up and go right to the couch, so she didn't end up paralyzed in bed. Then, she would have the television as a distraction. Annie didn't tell Michael that the television may have been on, but she couldn't pay attention to anything that was happening on the screen. She had found a psychiatrist that could see her in a week, and hoped for something other than Xanax to help her sleep. Maybe Paxil wasn't right to take anymore either.

Annie stopped trying to sleep during the day even when she was exhausted. Avery, on the other hand, was napping three times per day, so there wasn't a lot Annie could do to take her mind off of how she was feeling. It was milder than before, but Annie still couldn't stand living in her own body and the feeling increased as the day went on. It was like clockwork, which proved how hormonal the experience was. She would have a breakdown each day around three o'clock. Most of the time, she called her mother who she knew was already dealing with a lot at home, but was the only person who could calm her down. Her mother always encouraged her to take a shower, which did seem to help. By the time Michael would come home with Nicholas, Annie would feel notably better, although still dreading that she would have to get through another day. Each night she went to bed hopeful that the mornings would be better, but they were still a challenge.

Even so, her symptoms seemed to be slightly improving for the few days that she used the cream and started the estrogen patch, until they didn't. After one week of being on the Estrogen patch, Annie's entire being changed. It was like her pregnancy, but on steroids. She was agitated worse than she had been, and the bugs were back. When she had been pregnant with Avery, there was no morning sickness, she was sick all day and night. Michael urged her to find her old Zofran and take it, but Annie didn't know what was okay to take with the hormones she was taking.

Over the weekend, Annie had decided to take off the patch because it seemed to be amplifying her issues. She hadn't thought it could get any worse, but it had. She knew it would take a few days to get the estrogen out of her system, so she waited. It was Saturday when she had removed the patch, and now, Tuesday morning, she didn't even feel like she was connected to her body anymore. It was the first time in her life that she wanted to die. She really, truly would do anything to be put out of her misery.

There she was in Michael's arms being escorted to the couch ashamed of herself. She didn't want either of her children to ever look at her again. She was going to ruin them. If they felt even an ounce of her energy, they were going to be tainted forever. She couldn't think about anything except that she couldn't stand how she was feeling for a minute longer. It needed to end. "Michael, I want to die," she said aloud.

"Don't say that," Michael's voice was shaky. She couldn't remember when she had ever seen Michael cry. He was visibly scared for her.

It was the first time Annie understood why her father did what he did just two days before Christmas two years before. At the time, she had thought he was selfish and didn't care about the rest of the family, but that hadn't been true. Don hadn't wanted to be a part of the world anymore because he didn't want to ruin his children. He didn't feel like he could live with himself any longer. It was Don's first attempt.

Winnie had moved Don into an assisted living psychiatric facility. It provided a multitude of psychiatric services, but patients could come and go as they pleased. He hadn't done anything to pose himself as a true risk except make verbal comments about wanting to end his life. Winnie thought if he got the help he needed, he would be able to move back home and get back to his retired life. It was a beautiful facility that overlooked a small lake, surrounded by a walking trail, and the grounds were well kept. The dining room served better food than Winnie could cook, which wasn't saying much. It had been the perfect transition from the psychiatric facility Don had been in for a month and a half.

After his initial visit to the hospital to detox from Ativan, he had moved to a psychiatric facility because he wasn't medically stable. They needed to work out his medication and make sure he was on something that worked. However, they switched so many medicines so quickly, it was hard to tell if anything was truly working. On top of that, Don put on such a show for the doctors that according to them he was doing fine. Winnie would tell the girls that when the doctors left he would tell her that he wanted to die, and when the doctors would come in, he would tell them he was feeling good. Don had always been one to try and please everyone, and he never wanted to be a bother. It was only to Winnie that he felt he could place his burdens because he knew her love was unconditional and her loyalty forever.

The facility recommended Silver Lake as a next step for Don. It would be a place where he could have a psychiatrist, a therapist, groups to attend, and somewhere that he could regain his health. The place had excellent reviews and was well known for its services. It certainly cost enough. Winnie had felt relief the first night that he was there. She stayed for dinner with Don and the facility was throwing a small holiday party since it was just before Christmas. She even sent a picture of them dancing to the girls saying it was the best he had seemed since it all began. The whole family went to sleep that night feeling positive about the move for Don.

Annie was going to her in-laws for Christmas with Nicholas and Michael. They lived in Florida, so she had gotten on a plane early the next morning, still looking at the picture her mother had sent of her parents dancing. She hadn't seen her parents dancing since her wedding. Satisfied, she relaxed on the flight to Florida ready to enjoy some sunshine and the delectable cooking of her mother-in-law. Her in-laws had picked up the family in West Palm Beach and they were driving to their home in Port St. Lucie.

The drive had just begun when she received a call from Winnie. "Annie, where are you?" She didn't know why her mother always had to start this way with bad news. Her mother knew she didn't have a car with her, so she wasn't driving, and she knew that she was obviously not alone.

"We are in the car, Mom, what is it?"

"I have to tell you something."

Her father was dead. It was the call she had been waiting for since he had gone to the hospital the first time. Her hands were trembling, and her heart began beating fast, "What is it, Mom?"

"Your father is in the ICU."

"What happened?"

"Well, apparently after I left last night, he walked himself to the nearest pharmacy and bought a bottle of Tylenol. He went back to his room and took the whole bottle. His roommate heard him and went to get someone."

Annie hadn't even realized that her father had a roommate. "Is he conscious?"

"He's alive, Annie. He doesn't really know what's going on. The doctors don't know yet how much damage he's done to his liver. They don't know what's going to happen. I'm so sorry to tell you, Annie, but I couldn't..."

"Of course not, Mom. I would be angry if you didn't tell me." Annie was trying to hold it together. She hated to cry in front of other people, let alone her in-laws, whom after all this time, she still didn't feel completely comfortable around.

"Annie, I have to go, the doctor just came out."

"Okay, Mom," but Winnie had already hung up.

Annie couldn't hold it in any longer. She stared out the window watching the cars zoom by on I-95. She had always loved landing in Florida to visit her in-laws, looking around at the palm trees as they drove. This time, she just cried silently the entire drive, paying little attention to her surroundings. The whole car knew something had happened with her father, but no one wanted to ask. Michael knew better than to do so in front of his parents, knowing that Annie was not one to talk about her feelings publicly.

Don survived, despite his intentions, and spent a week in the ICU. He damaged his liver, but not to the point of never functioning again. Annie didn't remember anything about that trip to Florida except what happened with Don. She felt guilty that she was stuck far away, her mother insisting that she stay and not fly home, since Rye was already there and there was absolutely nothing anyone could do. When she talked to her father on the phone, he just sounded so sad.

"I did something really stupid, Annie. I did something really stupid. I didn't want to live anymore. I can't live like this. I just can't do it anymore. I was trying as hard as I could, and I just couldn't do it."

Annie had been a mix of sad and angry at her father. She couldn't imagine leaving her family behind, hurting them in that way. Didn't he love them enough to fight?

It was only now that she understood some sliver of what her father must have felt because she didn't feel like she had any fight left in her either. While she knew she would never do anything like that to herself or her family, she also didn't know what she was going to do. She couldn't care for her children. She couldn't be left alone.

Michael called in sick to work, increasing the shame she felt, but Michael couldn't stay home forever. He was an accountant and it was March. It was one of the busiest times of the year for him, and Annie knew he couldn't afford to take time away right now. Annie had taken off the remainder of the school year. Someone had to be out working. She could see Michael's panic, as he never even took a day off of work when he was sick. She heard him on the phone when she thought he was calling a coworker. "Hi Winnie," she overheard.

"NO!" she tried to scream, but it came out so quiet that Michael didn't even hear her.

"Winnie, we need you here. I know the timing couldn't be worse, but I don't know what else to do." Annie couldn't believe he was saying this to her mother. She felt complete shame that her mother would have to take care of both her and her father. Annie knew that her mother was already spread as thin as she could possibly be pulled. The next three hours were a blur as Annie waited for her mother to arrive. Michael spent most of the time holding her on the couch while she wept. He tried to get her to eat or drink something, but she couldn't. Annie couldn't even look at Avery. Michael took care of the daily routine even though he didn't know it. Normally, Annie would be correcting him and telling him what to do, but all she could do now was stare into space.

When her mom arrived, it was around eleven in the morning. "How are you here?" Annie asked.

"Well," her mother replied, "I hired Gordina for a reason, so I would be able to come and go. I didn't feel completely comfortable leaving her with your father, but it's only going to be for tonight, and then I'm going back."

Apparently, Michael and Winnie had talked other times throughout the morning, but she had been so dazed in her own mind she hadn't heard any of it. Michael had taken the next two days off of work, and she hadn't even realized. The two of them debated whether they should just take her to the hospital, but after her experience with Don, Winnie wasn't sure it would even be helpful.

Everyone was banking on the psychiatrist she was supposed to see that afternoon. It was only eleven and the appointment was at two, but Winnie told Annie to call the psychiatrist and see if he could get her in any earlier.

Annie called, her voice shaky and mousy. "Hi, Dr. Ruman? It's Annie. I was wondering if you could see me any earlier?"

"Isn't your appointment at two?"

"Yes"

"Well, that's only in three hours, how much earlier could you possibly come in?"

"I'm just really not doing well," she stammered.

"Do you have anything at home?

"What do you mean?"

"Anything you can take?"

"I have Xanax."

"I want you to take one of those, then take a shower, and then lie down until your appointment."

"Okay," Annie replied. She followed his instructions and laid in her bed. For the first time in days, she drifted off to sleep, but only for a few minutes.

Cade

Cade looked forward to when there was a celebration at school. It meant a lot of work for her, but it meant a change of routine too. It also meant that there would be a parent volunteer in her classroom. It was part of the school contract that parents were supposed to volunteer four hours per month at Blue River Charter School, but most of them didn't. Those who did come in, only came in for special occasions. The celebrations weren't like she remembered as a child, with maybe a box of cupcakes to pass out. The parents in this community came with goody bags and ice cream sundaes, and Cade was expected to make an afternoon out of it. She was meant to have extra recess, or show a movie, or do something special for the child. Then, there were the parents who didn't ever answer her phone calls or send their children in with a jacket, let alone plan out their birthdays at school. When it was these children's birthdays, it was up to Cade to make it special, because if one child had a celebration like that, they all needed to have one.

Cade had always loved her birthday as a child. Winnie always went above and beyond for birthday parties when the girls were younger. They were always at home, and never at some place that Winnie always referred to as a "party factory." Cade's birthdays included magicians that came to the house, scavenger hunts that her mother had organized, arts and crafts, balloon animals, a whole day devoted to each girl's birthday. There was always a theme, and Winnie seemed to look forward to the birthdays as much as her girls.

This was when she was younger. Now, Cade no longer liked her birthday. It had been ruined the past two years, and she had begun to believe it was bad luck for her family. The first year was when her father came covered in bruises only to spend the day of her birthday in the hospital. She couldn't believe no one woke her up to tell her. Her sisters were always treating her like the baby of the family, even though she was now a grown woman. The whole family looked back at the trip as where her father's downfall began. Unfortunately, the Adirondack Mountains was also a place they vacationed every summer and had for years. It was a family tradition. It wasn't just their family that went, but her entire mother's side of the family was there, including Aunt Vicki.

There was a part of all three sisters that blamed Aunt Vicki for Don falling down the stairs, even though it wasn't her fault. If she hadn't been there, he wouldn't have had so much to drink. Maybe he wouldn't have taken any extra Ativan, although deep down that they all knew this wasn't the cause. Don had been abusing Ativan for years, and he had been drinking too much for years.

Also, considering he had a mini seizure when he fell, there had to have been something else going on with him. He claimed he had been dehydrated and had played too much tennis in the sun, but the family would never really know because he had refused any medical care.

The following year the family returned for their annual family reunion, only this time without Don. It had started falling on Cade's birthday since she had been a teenager. They used to have it later in the summer, but then moved it to the first week of August permanently. When she was younger, this really bothered her, because what teenager wants to spend their birthday with their aunts and uncles? When she turned twenty-one this was really disappointing because her first legal drink was with her family. But this was the vacation they always took, and even though they had reservations about going back after the previous year, there they were.

Cade had hoped this birthday would be better than the year before. Don wasn't coming because he was at Willows. He had been there since March, and they didn't foresee him going anywhere else anytime soon. Winnie had signed a contract for him to be there for the year. After the incident where he took the bottle of Tylenol, and then two months later, when he drove his car into the lake, he couldn't be trusted anywhere that wasn't a completely supervised facility. She hoped that the family could enjoy themselves at least a little bit this time.

Winnie kept reminding them that they had to live their lives, and that's what their father would want.

Cade had recently seen her father at Willows and it was horrific. As soon as she walked in and smelled the urine seeping out of the walls, she began to cry to herself. When she saw her father, he immediately sobbed. He sobbed the whole time she was there, and she could barely make out his words. She had never seen another human being so incredibly sad. He also kept talking to her about the fact that he was going to jail. Winnie would snap at him that it wasn't true, and that if he was going to continue talking like that they were going to leave, but Cade could see that he truly believed it. It had been hard to understand her father because his words were so jumbled through his tears. He was slurring many words too, which may have been a side effect of all the medications he was taking, or a result of the deterioration of his brain that was taking place before their eyes with no explanation.

When they left, she asked her mother what he thought he was going to jail for since she wouldn't let him talk about it.

"Oh, it's nonsense," Winnie had said. "He had a patient who committed suicide years ago, and he thinks the family is going to sue him."

"Well, do they have any anger towards him?"

"No," Winnie replied in a huff. "They have never once contacted him, and he had nothing to do with it."

"Then why does he think he's going to jail for it?"

"Because he's not rational, Cade. He's not rational."

That was before Cade had moved out to North Carolina, but she hadn't flown home to visit since. She couldn't bring herself to go back to Willows. She didn't want to remember her father that way. It was beyond her comprehension how Winnie and Rye could visit him there every week. Nothing she had ever seen was more depressing. Winnie had told her that Cade's visit was one of the worst she'd ever seen him. Cade didn't know if that made her feel worse or better. At least her father wasn't like that all of the time, but he wasn't doing well. The place didn't seem to be helping him.

Her family was back at the Adirondacks that first week of August. Aunt Vicki kept asking how Cade was doing, but she couldn't help but hold a grudge towards her. Despite the fact that she knew her father's struggles went far beyond being disliked by Aunt Vicki, Cade couldn't help but hold anger towards her aunt for never liking her father, especially now. The week was going better than it had the year before. She had joined her sisters and their kids on boat rides, swam in the lake, hiked in the mountains, and relaxed on the porch looking out into the serene landscape.

It was a bit strange to be on a vacation that had always included her father. He had gone with them every year since she was little. He loved joining on the hikes, taking off his shoes, and wading in the small ponds at the top of the summits. He rented kayaks and paddled around Lake George. She and her father enjoyed drinks together, sitting in the rocking chairs on the porch, him asking her endless questions about school, her car, and boyfriends, genuinely interested in her answers. She tried not to think about where he was while they were all there—lying in a bed alone in a facility where he couldn't even leave the hallway without a nurse escort.

It was their last night in the Adirondacks when they got the call. Winnie came out looking frazzled talking on the phone. "Well what the fuck do you want me to do about it?" she asked frantically. "I'm not in town right now. I'm in the Adirondacks. You have to make the call." There was silence as the sisters watched their mother, hands flailing into the air. "I'm not there. How can I make the decision! Send him to the emergency room then. Haven't one of the nurses looked at him? Do what you think needs to be done." Winnie walked back into the building and sat down with her head in her hands.

All three sisters went to join her to find out what had happened. Rye was the first to speak, "Mom, what did they say?"

"Your father is going to the hospital again." Winnie didn't seem sad this time; she seemed angry, pissed off, livid. "I don't know what they want me to do about it from here. He knew we were here. He knew we were coming here this weekend. How could he do this?"

"Do what?" Annie asked.

Her father had attempted to kill himself for the third time. In a locked psychiatric facility where he supposedly was watched at all times, he had managed to attempt suicide, leaving himself seriously injured. He had found a piece of elastic from his jacket, pulled it out, and tied it around his neck. With the elastic wound around his neck, he had pulled as hard as he could until he passed out onto the floor. This was part of how they knew their father was losing his mind. It wasn't just depression. Their father was a genius. He was smart enough to know, or at least he had been intelligent enough to realize, that a person can't strangle himself. His hand would let go before he would die.

Unfortunately for Don, he had done more damage with this attempt than any other. In doing this to himself, he had given himself a stroke in two parts of his brain. He had lost the use of his left arm almost completely. The nurses had found him unable to move half of his body, and had called Winnie like she was going to be able to figure out what to do. There was nothing she could do. She had told them she would be home the next day, and the first stop she would make was the hospital.

Don was in the hospital for days, slowly regaining some feeling in the left side of his body, but still unable to use his hand or arm. He couldn't lift his arm to bathe himself or use his hand to zip up his own clothing. Don already couldn't stand being alive; he was completely unable to accept his diminished quality of life. Now, he had caused himself to be physically disabled. Although she felt selfish for thinking so, again Cade's birthday had been ruined. She couldn't help but feel irate at her father for doing this on her birthday during their family reunion. It turned out he had told the people at Willows that his family had left him and was never coming back. Cade's birthday was not only ruined, but she was beginning to realize that her father was really gone forever. He would never be the same man she knew. He was never going to recover from this.

Rye

All Rye had done was read the report. Her coworker had been absent the day of the meeting, and a special education teacher was needed to review the report. Her boss knew that she could look at a report quickly and be able to explain it, so she was the lucky chosen one. It was for an outplacement case, a child she had never met before in her life and would never see in the school building. Each teacher was given one of these each year, or at least they prayed it was only one. They were always a nightmare. The district was responsible for evaluating and planning a program each year for every student who was identified as requiring special education services, but was outplaced either by choice of the family or by the district. In this instance, Rye truly understood the phrase "no good deed goes unpunished."

This family was disgruntled with the entire evaluation. They weren't happy with the report Rye read, and they were especially unhappy with the report written by the psychologist. All that was stated were the facts. The child had told his teacher that, "He wasn't going to do this shit," and that "He fucking hated the lights in the building." When the assistant principal had introduced herself to him he had responded, "I don't give a shit." While the teacher hadn't written these exact words, she had written that he began the evaluation angry about the lights in the building and stating he wasn't going to do the work. The psychologist had to report his behavior at school, which was simply a summary of what had been given to her by the school he currently attended. The parents didn't want him portrayed in that light. They believed the evaluation was not a reflection of his true abilities even though he had performed just fine. The speech therapist, in their opinion, did not provide a comprehensive evaluation. They were suing the district and requesting that the district pay for an independent evaluation by an evaluator of their choice.

All Rye had done was read the report, yet there she was sitting with the district lawyer updating her resume because she would need it if she had to take the stand. She had to practice answering questions that she would be asked if she had to testify, resulting in hours of missed classroom time with her students. It was already impacting one of them, a generally perfectly well-behaved student with autism who always followed the rules, who had written, "SpongeBob is retarded" as his grammar sentence while she was wasting time in the conference room. While it had made her laugh (although not in front of him, especially when the student asked her to "please not tell his mom"), she knew that the time away from her students had a negative impact on their progress. She also knew that if she had to continue on as part of the case, the hours would exponentially increase, and she would be stuck in the conference room scrutinizing a report she didn't even write.

Most of the time that Rye was sitting with the lawyer, her mind wandered. The case really had nothing to do with her, and while her coworkers were anxious about whether they had evaluated properly, Rye couldn't stop thinking about her father coming home. It had been such a long two years for her, since she was the only one living close to her parents. She had accompanied Winnie to every emergency room, to every psychiatric facility, to Willows every Sunday, and it had worn on her.

In Rye's house, the chores were always done. She conducted her household by a strict routine. Her girls were well-behaved, and the house was run like a well-oiled machine. Will was always fixing something in the house, so everything was always in working order. If the house needed painting, he took care of it. When the toilet broke, he watched YouTube videos, went to Home Depot, and fixed it. From the outside, Rye's family looked picture perfect, and for the most part, they were as perfect as they come. Over the past two years, home was where Rye felt the most relaxed, the most at peace, the happiest.

No one, except her husband, knew that Rye had started taking Lexapro after the first emergency room visit with her father. She quietly scheduled an appointment with her primary care physician and got herself a prescription. After telling her doctor what she had just gone through with her father, it wasn't hard to get. Rye had never needed any medication in the past, and had always been fairly even-keeled, but after that incident she found herself waiting for the chips to fall. She was having trouble sleeping at night, which was impacting her ability to work to her normal level and parent the way she believed she should.

It wasn't anything that she was trying to keep secret, but Rye knew that she was viewed in a certain way in every aspect of her life. At work, she was the teacher given every difficult case because they believed she could handle anything. She was a previous teacher of the year, for Christ's sake. At home, she was the boss of the household, the one who held everything together. Everyone counted on her to make the decisions, to tell them what they should be doing and when. Now, being the one who lived closest to her parents, she was expected to be the representative for her sisters at all of the facilities where her father was being placed. It was she who had to run to every crisis because she had stayed close to home, and her sisters knew she could handle it.

Her sisters were always asking how her father was doing, and the answer was always difficult. The past two years had been a rollercoaster for Rye. While her mother had resigned herself to her father deteriorating, Rye still held out hope. Sometimes her father would give her glimmers of hope when she would visit. He was more open with Rye than her sisters. They had always been the closest. Growing up, Rye had been the one to take trips with her father. She was the only sister who shared his love of sports and enjoyed watching games with him. She was the most athletic of the three sisters, and she had been the only one who could play a game of tennis with her father, even though she always lost. Annie had always been closest with her mother, and Cade didn't seem to have a preference, but Rye was always very connected to Don.

When she would see Don in the hospital, he would confide in her. He would tell her that he wanted to die and share all of his delusions, like he would tell everyone else, but sometimes he would also tell her that he missed seeing her girls. Sometimes he would tell her that he watched part of a game on television for the first time in months. When she brought her father pictures of her girls to hang in his room at Willows, he seemed genuinely happy to see them.

It had been painful for Rye to see her father so distressed while he was detoxing. She didn't need him to be happy all of the time, but she wanted him to be calm. There were times when she went to visit him that he wasn't frantic and constantly talking about death. At the other extreme, he barely said a word to her, but she would take this as improvement and hope it meant he was heading in the right direction.

Rye just wanted to know what was wrong with him. Nothing had been clear. At first, it was a fall from an unknown reason. Then he was peeing blood, which turned out to be a real symptom of fairly progressed prostate cancer. He had abused benzodiazepines and gone through detox at the same time that his medications were changed so quickly and drastically that he experienced psychosis. He had received two different kinds of electroshock therapy, tried every medication that existed for depression and anxiety, and had been at the most renowned mental institutions in the country. Was it just an incredibly severe form of depression? Was it a brain injury from his fall? Had his cancer spread? Was he experiencing dementia?

The doctors that he saw completed thorough testing. He had a full medical workup to make sure his cancer hadn't spread to other parts of his body, especially his brain. Don had his prostate completely removed successfully. The family had taken him to highly recommended neurologists where he received testing for dementia, and it was declared he did not have this. He was an otherwise healthy man who had gone from living his life actively and fully to suddenly wanting nothing other than to die. He knew something was incredibly wrong with him, and whatever it was, he couldn't bear to live with it, but no doctor could find out what "it" was.

He was diagnosed with treatment-resistant depression. Rye didn't know this was even a real diagnosis, and it was the most hopeless diagnosis she had ever heard. When his prostate was removed, they found that the cancer had spread to his bladder neck, but to no other part of his body. It could easily be treated with radiation, but Don had no desire to receive the treatment. Rye constantly pushed for more tests and new methods of treatment. It was only because of Rye that Don had his prostate removed in the first place. He did it for her.

Now, Rye was worried about Don coming home. She didn't know if he was ready and if he was going to deteriorate further. She was glad that her mother had hired care for him and that nurses and an occupational therapist would be coming to the home. The nurse would make sure that he drank fluids to keep his blood pressure from dropping too low, which was another concern that constantly came up when he visited each doctor, but all chalked it up to dehydration. The occupational therapist was there to help him gain strength back in his left arm and hand. Since he gave himself a double stroke, he was unable to dress and bathe himself without help. Though her mother described the visits with the occupational therapist as throwing around a balloon that he would be asked to practice doing with Gordina, Rye hoped it was helping him.

Rye had only been to visit once in his first week home, but she had to admit that Don was looking the best he had in two years. Yes, he laid in bed most of the time, but when he wasn't, there was color back in his face. He was clean shaven, and his nails were cut unlike when he was at Willows and she couldn't stand to look at his growing beard and long nails that no one cared for when they knew he couldn't do it himself. His sheets were getting changed on a regular basis, his clothes washed after each wear, and he was bathing at least every other day. He wasn't happy, and he barely spoke two words to her while she was there, but he looked better. He looked healthier.

When she had visited, Winnie told her about Annie. Rye didn't know why her sister never reached out to her. She had two kids of her own, and while she hadn't experienced postpartum depression, she wanted to be there for her sister. She tried calling Annie every day after seeing Winnie, but Annie wouldn't answer. She left messages telling Annie that she was thinking of her and knew she was having a hard time, but Annie never even answered her through text message. She hoped everything was fine. She couldn't take anymore crises.

Rye was jolted back to reality as the lawyer flew back into the conference room after lunch. She had spoken to the family's lawyer while they were eating, and they decided that Rye need not be part of the case. The only perk to being part of a lawsuit was that everyone ordered lunch. Rye quickly finished her sandwich, and then returned to her classroom. Being in the classroom had become one of the only parts of her life where she felt in control.

Winnie

She could barely look at her daughter; the look was all too familiar. Winnie was staring at her daughter in complete despair, completely disheveled in a way she didn't know her daughter could look. When she arrived, Annie was still in her pajamas. She was laying on the couch, pale and sunken in. She hadn't seen Annie in a couple of weeks, and she had clearly lost weight. Her daughter had been blessed with beautiful curls that she usually, against Winnie's best wishes, neatly straightened or tied back in a bun. Today, her daughter looked like she hadn't brushed or washed her hair in a week.. It was everywhere, puffed out from her head. It looked like she had taken a hairbrush and just brushed the curls in all different directions.

Michael looked relieved to see Winnie, and his eyes were pleading for her to say something because, although Michael was a devoted and loving husband, he didn't always have the words. There had been a part of Winnie that was looking forward to coming even though she wished it was under better circumstances. She scooped up her beautiful granddaughter, nuzzling her fuzzy, bald head and breathing in the sweet scent of baby soap and lotion. Winnie oohed and aahed over how much Avery had changed, hoping she could engage her daughter, but

Annie's eyes were blank. She just stared in the direction of her fireplace even though the television was on in front of her above it. Michael had put on the shows she liked to watch, where houses were being renovated or picky buyers were choosing their perfect home, but Annie wasn't watching.

Winnie put down Avery and went to stroke Annie's head, smelling the stench of vomit that radiated off of her breath and hair. "This too shall pass," she reminded her daughter. "You've been through this before, you'll do it again."

Tears streamed down Annie's face. "This time is different, Mom. This time is different. I can't live like this."

Michael had called Winnie telling her he was extremely worried about Annie. He had hated to bother her, knowing that it wasn't easy for Winnie to leave at the current moment. In fact, up until she received the call, Winnie had considered staying overnight an impossibility. Michael had told her that Annie was worse than he had ever seen her, that she couldn't function as a mother at the moment, and that he couldn't leave her alone, but Winnie didn't realize how dire the situation really was.

Hearing her daughter speak like that brought up too many emotions for Winnie. She had spent the past two years hearing how her husband wanted to end his own life. She couldn't hear this from her daughter. Her beautiful, energetic, cheerful, and friendly daughter who was always the life of the party, lying there saying she couldn't go on. Although it was painful, she was glad she came. Her daughter needed her and seemed determined to feel better. Don was complacent in his recovery, or lack thereof, but Annie wanted to be there for her family.

Winnie had set up everything for Gordina at home. She had prepped all of Don's food for the night and the next day, even though Gordina said she was perfectly capable of prepping his meals. She had called to reschedule the nurse visit for the following afternoon when she knew she'd be home. She liked to be there when the nurses or occupational therapist came to visit because sometimes they gave Don instructions, and he was not reliable relaying information. Gordina listened too, but her English wasn't fluent, so she sometimes missed part of what they were saying as well.

Then, Winnie had called Rye. "Rye, your sister is in trouble."

"What's wrong?" Rye asked with alarm.

"I don't know exactly, but Michael called that she is experiencing severe postpartum depression. He didn't trust her to be alone with the baby, and he's taken the day off of work."

Rye knew that Michael didn't take time off of work, especially during tax season. "Do you need me to come with you, Mom?" Rye asked.

"No, I need you to help me with your father."

"Whatever you need. What can I do?"

"I need you to come over and check on him once this afternoon while I'm gone."

"Is that it? Do you want me to stay there?"

"No, honey. I just need someone to check in."

"Do you not trust Gordina?"

"Honey, I barely know her. She's been in the house a week. I will just feel more comfortable if I know that someone is going to be checking in at the house."

"Okay, that's no problem. I'll head there right after work today."

"Thank you, Rye." She knew Rye had enough on her plate, but she also knew she could always count on her. While she still didn't feel completely confident leaving Don, she didn't know what else to do.

Her phone rang, and it was Gordina. Winnie's heart sank. What now? How could Don do anything now when his own daughter was in crisis? Winnie had told Don what was going on with Annie, not in great detail, only that Annie needed her. Don could infer given what had happened after Nicholas was born, and had told her that she should definitely go. Was this just a manipulation for her to leave the house, so he could do something stupid?

"I have to take this," Winnie said as she quickly left the room. "Gordina, what is it? Is everything alright?"

"Oh yes, ma'am. We just went out for our daily walk, and Don is now lying down. I just wanted to make sure you made it there okay." Winnie felt tears well in her own eyes. It was the first time someone had checked on her well-being in a long time. She had been taking care of everyone and everything for so long, she had forgotten what it felt like.

Gordina didn't know the reason she was visiting, and thought that her daughter simply needed help with the baby. "Oh yes, everything is just fine. The baby is beautiful as can be, and I'm going to go back and hold her right now."

"Wonderful ma'am. What time can we expect you tomorrow?"

"I'll be home in the early afternoon, Gordina. Thank you for all your help."

"No problem, ma'am. I will look forward to seeing you tomorrow."

She didn't know why she had been so worried. Gordina had it all under control. This was why she had hired her, wasn't it? It was why she had let a stranger move into her house and take over her bedroom, living room, and kitchen. It was time to focus her attention on her daughter, and Annie wasn't okay. It was one thing to watch Don go through this pain, but seeing it in her daughter was like feeling the pain herself. In fact, she wished she could take Annie's pain as her own. She would if she could.

It had been her idea to call the psychiatrist earlier. She knew that the appointment was only in a few hours, but she didn't think she could watch Annie suffer like this for even three more hours. When the doctor gave her the advice to take a Xanax and a shower, she had concerns. It was going to take more than a shower for her daughter to get better. She had lost faith in the mental health system after Don and was worried the road would be just as bumpy for Annie.

As her daughter went upstairs, following the doctor's orders, Winnie did the only thing she knew to do. She picked up the baby again and began rocking her, singing, "Avery is a good girl, yes she is. I love Avery, yes I do." She stared into Avery's innocent eyes as they began to slowly close. Winnie sat down where Annie had laid all morning and rested the baby on her chest. She closed her eyes and prayed for a miracle.

Annie

Annie recognized the building immediately. She had been there a week before to meet with a recommended therapist. The therapist met with her for an hour and didn't charge her. Annie told her all she was feeling physically and what she had experienced after Nicholas. She told the therapist that she had just started hormone therapy, because this was before she removed the patch, and that she had an appointment with Dr. Ruman the following week. The therapist had told her that she didn't think there was anything for them to discuss further unless Annie wanted to come there just to talk. She just had to let the hormonal wave ride its course.

"But what do I do in the meantime?" she asked.

"You take care of yourself." God, Annie hated when people said this. She was a mother of a newborn baby. There was no "taking care of yourself." Up until that point, her entire body had been devoted to caring for her baby. Caring for yourself meant taking a shower. It wasn't like someone was watching the baby while she went to have her nails done or get a massage, but Annie didn't want to be rude, so she said nothing at all.

She agreed that there was no reason to come back and visit this therapist. She was surprised she had come so highly recommended from her gynecologist. Just like the first time, Annie couldn't find anyone who really seemed to validate what she was going through and offer any helpful suggestions for strategies that would actually help her through this time. Annie couldn't wait it out. There were two humans to take care of in her home. Sure, she could follow the advice to let the laundry go, and then increase her stress that it wasn't done. She could ask Michael for more help, but he was already working full time to support the family, and he helped where he could when he was home.

The therapist had made her nervous for her visit with the psychiatrist. "You are going to see Dr. Ruman, huh?" she asked in a way that made her seem intrigued.

"Yes," she had replied skeptically.

"What made you choose him?"

"He had excellent reviews online."

"I would be interested to hear how you find him," she had said.

"What is that supposed to mean?"

"He's an interesting man, that's all. Unconventional. Just make sure you don't pay him his full asking price." It was true that when she called, Dr. Ruman had told her that his rate was three hundred dollars in cash, no exceptions, and he didn't take any insurance. "Tell him you don't have the money and need to work out a deal."

Annie knew she probably wouldn't do that. She wasn't very good at that kind of negotiating. She wasn't going to change her appointment. Online, the reviews had said that Dr. Ruman was life changing, that he went above and beyond for his patients. This is the kind of doctor she needed. Maybe unconventional would be better than the typical care she was receiving since none of it was helping her.

Annie rode the elevator past the floor of the therapist she had seen to the very top. Both Michael and Winnie had come to the appointment. Michael was going to go in with her, and Winnie was going to watch the baby in the waiting room. Thankfully, the family could attend the appointment while Nicholas was still at daycare. Annie wasn't quite sure why her mother didn't just stay home with the baby, but she appreciated all of the support. They sat on chairs with red, scratchy cushions, and Annie stared at the painting on the wall. It was an abstract art painting that also included pieces of fabric. It was also different shades of red, which Annie found distasteful as a room full of red didn't seem to provide the calmness she would expect to feel when seeing a psychiatrist or therapist. There were noise machines like the ones her children used whirring outside of other doors to protect the confidentiality of the people inside. Dr. Ruman was the only psychiatrist. The rest of the offices were for licensed social workers.

Annie felt weak and pathetic waiting in the waiting area. She hadn't eaten a meal in days, and while it hadn't been as long as it seemed, she couldn't remember when she last held her daughter. Winnie picked up Avery out of the car seat and held her. Annie looked away, ashamed that she still didn't want anything to do with her baby. She heard footsteps coming down the hallway and a man peeked into the waiting room. He was wearing a suit, and his shoulders were almost completely hunched over. It looked like it was difficult for him to walk. When he stood, the top of his head was visible because his back was so rounded, and it exposed his greasy, parted hair. He wore glasses that he pushed up with his finger as he looked at the family. He was an older man, probably in his seventies. "Oh, you brought the whole family," he said in a calm, quiet voice. "Annie, right? Follow me."

Annie and Michael followed Dr. Ruman into an office that was not what she expected. She had envisioned a room with a comfortable couch, where she would lie down and spill her feelings. Dr. Ruman's office had a large desk that he sat behind, and two uncomfortable metal chairs. To the side of the office was a large bookshelf filled with medical books and journals along with a card made by his grandchildren. There was a small clock sitting on one shelf that could be seen by both doctor and patient. On the other shelf was a pile of snacks that Dr. Ruman ate throughout the day. Behind him, a wall was covered with framed degrees. The office had a large window that overlooked the street. Annie watched the cars whizzing by down below.

"So, tell me what's going on," Dr. Ruman began. He pulled out a yellow legal pad and she watched him write her name and the date at the top.

Annie immediately began to cry. "Well, I am experiencing postpartum depression, but I'm already on Paxil."

"Who prescribes your Paxil?"

"My obstetrician."

"Any how many milligrams are you taking of that?"

"Now I'm taking thirty, but before I only took twenty."

"And how are you doing that?"

"I cut the second pill in half and take one and a half." Dr. Ruman was writing down her every word.

"How are you sleeping?"

"I'm not sleeping. That's one of the biggest problems." She went on to tell Dr. Ruman about each physiological symptom she was experiencing along with hopelessness, anxiety, and sadness that she felt.

He asked extremely specific questions about her daily routine such as when she woke up, when she ate her first meal, whether she exercised during the day, and what she engaged in before bed. He asked strange questions like how she was as a student when she was younger, what her son's personality was like, if she was generally a dramatic person. Here and there, Michael chimed in with additional information that Annie had forgotten to divulge. Annie found it helpful to have him there, so that

Dr. Ruman would know that this truly deviated from how she usually felt and acted. Dr. Ruman filled pages and pages of notes as Annie spoke. Many of his questions seemed irrelevant, but he asked them seriously, so she answered them in the same manner.

Dr. Ruman then pulled out a few of his books, and looked at certain pages. He didn't say anything for a very long time. She would have expected a doctor to give information about what it is they were looking up, or to at least say, "hold on a minute." It was only about five minutes, but it felt much longer as they sat in the room in complete silence. She alternated between watching the clock, looking out the window, and wiping her eyes with a tissue Dr. Ruman had handed her when she had begun crying. Dr. Ruman then pulled out a prescription pad, and he began writing her prescriptions.

"I am going to put you on Lithium…" Annie didn't let him finish. Lithium? All she knew about Lithium was from Rye. Rye would talk about her emotionally disturbed students who took Lithium. She knew that this was a drug for people with severe mood disorders such as bipolar disorder.

"I'm not taking Lithium," she declared.

"I think it would be the most helpful at this time for you," Dr. Ruman explained, again in a calm and warm demeanor. "I don't expect you to take this for a long time, but we need something to break the cycle."

"But that's a drug that emotionally disturbed people take." She was immediately embarrassed for saying this.

Dr. Ruman disregarded the judgmental comment. "Lithium can be very helpful for people who are in a state of severe anxiety and depression when nothing else is working. You will be on a very low dose, the lowest dose possible. I will need you to go get your blood drawn within the next couple of days. When taking Lithium, you need to have your blood taken in order to make sure it is not impacting your kidney function and to check your blood levels."

Annie did not want to take this drug, but she agreed to take the prescription. "I'm also going to prescribe you trazodone for sleep, and I'm going to give you a prescription for one hundred and twenty Xanax."

"But isn't Xanax addicting?"

"You aren't going to take it indefinitely. I want you to have it because over the next few days, I want you to take it when you are feeling agitated. We need to get you feeling better."

"How am I supposed to be able to drive? What if I need to get something?"

"Who can help you?" Michael chimed in that he would be taking the next couple of days off of work, but did admit that they didn't have a plan past that point.

"You need to find someone who can help you for the next couple of weeks. You shouldn't be alone, and you need to be able to sleep when you are able."

Annie took the prescriptions and brought them out to her mother. Winnie was also surprised to hear that she would be taking Lithium. Don had tried Lithium, and Winnie didn't see Annie that way, or, at least, she didn't want to see her that way. She didn't want her to be in such a severe episode that she would need such a strong drug to help her, but she was just as desperate for her daughter to feel better.

When they got home, Annie took the medicine right away. She was to take one in the evening and one in the morning. She also took her trazodone right away, and left the family to go to bed while it was still light out. Her mother was going to take Avery downstairs for the night. Michael was going to take care of Nicholas, and her only job was to sleep. Annie laid in bed for over an hour, but she didn't feel restless. Sleep just wasn't coming. But then it did, and Annie slept for nine hours for the first time since before Avery was born.

Cade

"Well-distinguished in that category. You bring dahversitay to our school!" Ms. Jay exclaimed in her southern accent.

Cade wasn't sure how she brought diversity anywhere. She was a white girl from Fairfield County, Connecticut. It didn't really get less diverse than that. She looked at Ms. Jay quizzically. Mrs. Jackson went on, "Well, I mean, ya had the kids playing dreidel, learning all about your heritage…" She trailed off a bit nervously.

Cade thought back to the holidays at Blue River Charter School. In every other way, the school was so progressive. It was like a little bubble placed in the middle of a stereotypical rural, poor southern town. However, when the holidays came, even Blue River Charter School couldn't hide that it was south of the Mason Dixon Line.

Ms. Jay had come into her room before the day had started. "Cade, I'm popping into each room this morning reminding everyone to think about what they want to do for the holidays. We've always done an ornament exchange, but maybe we want to do something different this year."

"Well, I guess I'd vote to do something different this year because I don't know exactly what I'd do with an ornament."

"What on earth do you mean?"

"Well, I'm Jewish, Ms. Jay. I don't have a Christmas tree at home."

"Oh my, I didn't realize." Ms. Jay was visibly embarrassed. She prided herself in being inclusive, accepting of diversity, culturally sensitive.

"It's okay," Cade had reassured. "I just would probably rather do something else."

Many of her students lived with relatives because their parents were in rehabilitation facilities or jail. One of the grandmothers who was a guardian of one of Cade's students approached her about bringing in a Christmas tree into the classroom for the holidays. Cade was absolutely shocked that anyone would dream of putting a Christmas tree inside a public school classroom. Although they were a charter school, they were still publicly funded. Hadn't this woman ever heard of separation of church and state? The grandmother got frustrated and annoyed with Cade telling her that far too much had changed in schools since she was younger. Cade tried to explain that if she celebrated Christmas, she would then need to celebrate every other holiday to be sure she didn't exclude anyone.

Her teaching assistant went behind her back and made a handprint Christmas tree on the bathroom door. Cade saw her calling over students in the morning, but she thought it was to tell them something about their homework folders. She was too busy each morning ushering students into the classroom, getting them started on their morning work, and meeting with students about homework they had trouble with from the night before, to notice what her assistant was doing. When Cade confronted her about it, her assistant said she couldn't bear for the kids to not have a Christmas tree in the room. Her assistant also told her that meeting her had shown her that people different from her could still be good people, a shocking statement inconsistent with the values of the school.

Cade gave in, but decided that she would make sure that the students learned that Christmas wasn't the only holiday celebrated. She taught them about Hanukkah and Kwanzaa too. Cade knew that she was still leaving many cultures out, but she at least exposed them to the fact that there were people different from them in the world. She knew she had to when she sat down for a mid-year conference and the parent said, "So, Julia tells me that you celebrate Kwanzaa. How lovely."

Her students knew very little beyond their trailer parks. They knew she was from Connecticut and one had asked, "Ms. Cade, how long does it take you to get here from Connecticut every day?" She told them that she had grown up close to New York City, and a child said he had once been there. As his family who lived there was solely Spanish speaking, he asked, "Ms. Cade? You from Connecticut? Does that mean you speak Spanish?" Since many of them couldn't afford fruit and vegetables, they were shocked by the food she ate. One student had never seen a cucumber, another a plum, and many were completely disgusted as she ate hummus in front of them for lunch. She had them grow their own chickpea plants to show them what it was made from.

Cade felt it was necessary that the school worked to provide the students with a diverse education. Even though they had been sent there by their families, many sent them there because they knew the test scores were higher. She learned this when one of the white girls in her class refused to hold the hand of a black student when Cade was teaching a music lesson and having them do a dance. "My grandma says you shouldn't touch black people." Cade had explained to the student why this was wrong, but as hard as she tried in the classroom, she couldn't undo what a child was taught by her family. However, the girl never made another racist comment in her classroom again.

While Cade didn't agree that it warranted a higher score on her evaluation, it was the first time she had taken pride in being Jewish. Don had always wanted his girls to grow up celebrating their faith. Winnie, on the other hand, didn't believe in organized religion. She believed in a higher being, but not in the traditions and strict beliefs that were required when practicing a religion. Since she was the one who spent most of the time raising the children while Don worked, most of them were shaped by her beliefs instead.

Annie was the only one who had a Bat Mitzvah, which made her father very proud. Rye had always been so close with her father, that he never seemed to push his religious beliefs on her in the same way he did Cade. Somehow, maybe because they shared such an interest in sports, Rye had gotten away with not finishing Hebrew school, or maybe it was because she was the oldest. By the time Cade came around, Don was not willing to back down so easily. She was required to go to Hebrew school, which she found both boring and humiliating. A bus would pick her up and take her there after school, and she would have to ride with three very strange children to the synagogue. None of her friends were Jewish, and she felt like she didn't fit in.

When Cade was in the sixth grade, she decided to go on strike. If her father called from work to check in, she would ignore him and pass the phone right off to her mother. When she started having to go to a Hebrew school tutor because dance took up too much time in the evenings, she would just refuse to complete the work assigned. When the tutor complained to her father and both looked to her for an answer, she remained silent. Cade felt pure hatred towards her father for making her go to Hebrew school, and if she was going to have a Bat Mitzvah, it would have to be over her dead body. It wasn't happening.

Eventually, Don caved in and let her stop going, much to his dismay. Now, again, Cade felt like she didn't fit in, but it wasn't just because she was Jewish. That may have been what caused her to stand out at work, but with her friends, she seemed to be the odd man out too. While she enjoyed all of the festivals of bluegrass, barbecue, and beer, and she looked forward to the weekends to go out dancing at a bar, she wasn't like the friends she had made. Their friendship was superficial, and mostly because she had no one else.

They always got ready together before they went out, but Cade arrived thinking she was ready. Cade never did much to get ready besides wash and dry her hair, and maybe throw on a bit of mascara. She already had rosy cheeks dotted with freckles that others had always described as "cute." She had bright blue eyes and a big, easy smile that had always drawn in others. Her figure was slim and fit, a dancer since she was five years old. She threw on a dress and a pair of nicer looking flip flops and called it a day. Not her friends; they curled their hair for hours, filling her lungs with hairspray. They globbed on makeup, layer after layer. Their high heels made Cade's feet hurt just looking at them. To go to an outdoor festival, they were dressed better than Cade would be for a wedding. She was surprised they even wanted to be out in public with her, and she understood why they were always trying to get her to borrow their clothing. Sometimes she did, so she would look more like the group, but she didn't feel herself.

Her relationship with Ryan wasn't going that well anymore either. They had only known each other a few months before she moved in the first place. It was an instant connection, as their mutual friend introduced them. It made life easy. They already had the same friends, enjoyed the same activities, and were surprised they hadn't met earlier. If Ryan didn't have another year to finish in graduate school, they would have moved out to North Carolina together. She really believed he would have come with her; they were already saying they loved each other just weeks into the relationship. In the fall, she had gone to visit Ryan, staying a whole week. It had been a perfect week of seeing her old friends and forgetting about work for the first time since the year had started. Even Ryan mentioned how nice it was to hear her talking about something else.

She had also seen Ryan over the holidays, but only briefly, as she spent most of the break with her family. Ryan had come to her house just for one night to see her. Her mother hadn't been fond of him. She didn't think he seemed all that interested in Cade and her life. He didn't talk much during dinner with them, but Cade thought maybe he was being shy. Since that visit, the relationship had been strained.

Ryan seemed to be missing her calls more frequently and taking more time than usual to call her back. When they did talk on the phone, if Cade tried to talk about work, Ryan quickly tried to change the subject. He was clearly sick of hearing about it. He never asked how her father was doing, and seemed genuinely uninterested in her life. If she brought up that things seemed different between them, he would say he was stressed about his graduate work or that he was tired, but Cade could feel him slipping away.

Cade had been in North Carolina less than a year, but she was beginning to long for home. She didn't know how much longer she could maintain the energy needed to do her job each day. Most mornings, she dreaded getting out of bed because she knew what awaited her as soon as she did. An hour long commute, an hour of setting up, a day with no breaks and constant fires to put out all by herself, two hours of organizing her classroom for the next day, and then another hour drive home all in just one day. What if she ever wanted to have a family? She didn't even have time for herself. She would never be able to live the life she envisioned doing this job. Maybe it was time for a change.

Rye

She hurried Emilie and Carter into the car. She thought it best to leave Will home, as it might be too much for Don. There was no rush to get over to her parents' house, but Rye was a mix of nerves and excitement. Winnie had come back from Annie's house, and Don had agreed to see the grandchildren. It was the first time he would be seeing any of his grandchildren in over a year. He had refused to see any of them, but now that he was home, Winnie wanted to be able to have her family over. It may have been Winnie's push, but she said that Don was going to come out of his room and see them. Don hadn't even come out to see Rye when she once visited Don alone.

It was a big step for Don. Rye had gone over to visit Don while Winnie had been away, and when she came in, she didn't really know what she was doing there. Don was lying in bed and only answered her with nods or shakes of his head.

"Dad, can I get you anything?"

Head shake.

"Did you already go for a walk today?"

Head nod.

"Do you want to come out of bed?"

Head shake.

She had sat for a while in the living room making small talk with Gordina ,who seemed like a lovely woman, but then she found herself thinking about all she needed to be doing at home. There was no point sitting on a couch there when she should be home tending to the girls, the chores, making food, and all that kept Rye busy in her daily life. She knew that Don wouldn't want her sitting there staring at him. So, she had told her mother that all seemed to be status quo and left.

Now that Winnie was back, Rye was anxious to hear how Winnie's visit had gone with Annie because Annie still wasn't returning her phone calls. She wasn't sure why Annie was doing this because Rye had never considered herself to be judgmental of Annie in the past. Annie had made comments before about how "together" Rye always appeared. Maybe she thought that Rye wouldn't understand. She knew that Annie had some resentment towards her, but she wasn't sure why.

When Rye came into the house, this time with her girls, Don was already sitting at the kitchen table having a drink. He seemed to be looking better and better each time she saw him even if he was lying in bed most of the time. Compared to her visits to Willows, her father looked like a different human being. It was a beautiful spring day, and Winnie suggested they go outside and play a little game of catch. Rye felt nervous for her father. Would he be able to physically throw and catch a ball, or would she feel embarrassed for him?

She hadn't talked to Emilie and Carter about Don before they arrived. They had known that their grandpa was sick and had been somewhere for a long time, but she didn't tell them details. She still didn't even know exactly what the details were, so she told them all she knew; that grandpa was sick. She hadn't prepared them for playing catch with her father, so when she saw how gently they were passing the ball and running to get it when he missed a catch, it brought tears to her eyes.

Emilie kept holding his hand just for a second or two and then would run away again to get the ball and throw it. Carter kept making sure her passes were calm and easy, and would say, "Ready Grandpa?" before tossing the ball lightly to him. The girls didn't seem bothered by the fact that their grandpa looked different since they last saw him. He had lost a significant amount of weight, his shoulders were much more hunched over, and he had little use of his left hand. Don was left-handed, so trying to catch with his right hand would have been difficult even if his physical functions were intact.

They all sat down to dinner, and it was the first time Don didn't talk about getting arrested, or Winnie leaving him, or his bodily functions. He didn't say much of anything, but he tolerated sitting at the dinner table while her girls stole the conversation. They wanted to tell their grandpa all of the random details of their lives. Emilie told about the bad word her friend said on the playground, that she wished she was a butterfly, and sang the song she was practicing for the end of the year chorus performance. Carter told him what she was learning about in school, her favorite book, and that her softball team had won their last game. Neither one seemed to mind that Don did little more than grunt in response to them. They just kept on talking.

"So, Mom, how was Annie?"

"Oh honey, she's not well. I feel very guilty that I'm not still there."

"Is anyone with her?" Rye asked.

"Well, Michael took the next couple of days off of work, so it felt silly for us both to be there, and he called his mother to come," Winnie explained.

Rye almost choked on the carrot she had just put in her mouth. "His mother is coming? For how long?" Rye knew how Annie felt about her mother-in-law. It wasn't that she didn't like her, but she felt very judged by her. She wasn't comfortable around her. Her mother-in-law was a classy lady who enjoyed the finest of everything, whereas Annie was simple. Annie's idea of a dinner was spaghetti with meatballs, and Michael's mother served better food than she had ever eaten at a restaurant. Annie was a liberal Democrat who kept her political opinions to herself, and her mother-in-law was a diehard Republican who loved to talk politics. Annie always described her as a loving, generous, and thoughtful woman, but she would also tell Rye that she would get anxious before they would visit in Florida. She always worried she was going to do or say something wrong in the house or accidentally speak her mind about politics.

"I know, Rye. I know that it might not be easy for Annie, but Susan wanted to come. She hasn't even met the baby yet, and I think Michael needs her too. This isn't easy for him either"

"I know, Mom, but is Annie okay with it?"

"Honey, she has to be. The doctors say she can't be alone right now, and she can't drive, so someone has to be there with her. The worst thing that happens is she eats a few gourmet meals and has to hear about Donald Trump."

Rye felt guilty that maybe she should go help Annie, but she knew she couldn't leave her kids or her job. Spring was a busy time at work for her. It was the time most of her yearly meetings took place, and she had a lot to prepare. There would be numerous additional meetings just to plan the program they would be proposing for each student. She would be on the phone with parents continuously so there were no surprises when they all came to the table. No, this was not a time that Rye could get away.

Even though Annie was having a hard time, Rye left Winnie's that night feeling hopeful. Don had participated with the family more than he had in over a year. Even if all he could do was be present at family gatherings, maybe he would slowly begin to improve. Maybe he needed to hit rock bottom, and now he was getting the help he needed. Rye left that night feeling lighter than she had in years.

Winnie

Don immediately retreated to his room after Rye left, after first obsessing to Winnie that he couldn't pee or poop. Even she had believed for a moment that Don was improving. Sure, it was the first time he had agreed to see his grandchildren, and he did interact with them more than he had with anyone, besides telling Winnie about his delusions. However, Winnie had learned what Don's silence meant, and he had been silent during most of the visit. It didn't mean that he was calm. It meant that he was extremely anxious and obsessing about his thoughts to the point that it paralyzed him. He was unable to speak because he was too absorbed in his own mind to talk to anyone else unless they wanted to hear the tape he played in his head over and over again.

Winnie was drained after coming back from Annie's house. She felt guilty for leaving Annie in the state that she was in, but she didn't see the point of staring over her and Michael if he was going to stay home with her. Winnie had taken Annie to the hospital to get her blood drawn the morning before she left. Some of the color had come back to her face, and although messy, her hair was at least pulled back. She had been able to pull herself together enough to get dressed and make it to the appointment.

Annie seemed distant when she was there even when they sat right next to each other. It seemed like her mind was on another planet. Winnie wasn't sure if it was from lack of sleep, her new medication, or both. She didn't like Annie being on Lithium and worried whether they should be trusting Dr. Ruman. He seemed strange to Winnie, which didn't necessarily mean he wasn't competent, but she wasn't sure she trusted him. Then again, she didn't trust any doctor after what she had experienced trying to get help for Don. Annie said he listened to her, which was more than Winnie could say for any doctor Don saw.

It had been stressful for Winnie to be away from Don. While she appreciated Gordina checking in, each phone call caused her stomach to do somersaults. Every time, she thought it was going to be like the many calls she received before. It was clear to her that she didn't trust Don being home, and she felt responsible for what he did. She was worried her children would never forgive her for taking him home if he attempted suicide again, especially if he was successful.

Michael called his mother against Annie's wishes. She was flying in from Florida and was staying for a week. Annie certainly did not need both mothers hovering over her. Besides, Winnie thought it might be good for their relationship. She knew that there were aspects of Susan that Annie found intimidating, and she had trouble relaxing completely around her, but maybe spending this much time together would cause that to change, or it would be a disaster. Also, Susan hadn't met Avery yet, and this would give her plenty of time to be with the baby because Annie needed to be sleeping and relaxing every chance she got. Winnie also knew that Susan was an impeccable chef, and Annie hadn't eaten a real meal in weeks. Maybe it would put some meat back on her bones.

Winnie hoped the medications worked because she couldn't fathom Annie going through what Don had gone through the past two years. Each place he went switched his medications, waited a few days, and then switched them again. Since there was no place that knew his baseline, they didn't believe Winnie when she would tell them that he was acting psychotic, telling lies, or acting beyond agitated. Don was a quiet, introverted man, so since his behavior wasn't overtly psychotic, he was viewed as improving.

Winnie would never forget being there when Don received his electroshock therapy. The psychiatric facility already felt spooky to her. Even though it was surrounded by trees, planted flowers, and a brook that ran behind the building, she felt queasy every time she visited. In order to get to the electroshock therapy room, Don had to be taken through a tunnel that ran through the basement of the building. As the elevator doors opened, she felt like she was taking Don to his death.

The doctors and nurses were kind and reassuring, but Winnie couldn't help picturing *One Flew Over the Cuckoo's Nest*. Winnie wasn't allowed in the room while

Don had the procedure, and she was thankful for this rule. She didn't think she could watch the procedure being done. She imagined Don so helpless and scared as he waited for the anesthesia to take over. Winnie went to the psychiatric facility every time Don had to have the procedure, so she could be there when he got to recovery.

Don received both unilateral and bilateral electroshock therapy, as the unilateral had not led to any improvement. The bilateral led to expected memory loss, and Don often seemed a bit confused after these treatments. Winnie worried about what this was doing to his cognitive functioning. She didn't know whether this contributed to his inability to read anything. She wondered if it was why he couldn't focus on anything while watching television, which used to relax him after work. There was no way for her to know because all Don talked about was how badly he wanted to die.

Winnie feared for Annie, and she knew that Annie had the same fear. Annie was in a severe episode of postpartum depression and Winnie knew it would be a long haul for her to get back to herself. "Mom, what if I never get back to myself?"

"Oh honey, you will. This is a severe postpartum episode, but it's going to pass. You're going to get through it. This too shall pass."

"When?"

"I don't know, honey, but you will. You need to focus on the small moments when you don't feel terrible." Just that morning, Annie had realized that it was Avery's two-month birthday. She got off of the couch for the first time all morning, dressed her baby up in the cutest outfit she had, adding the final touch of a sweet bow, and took a two-month-old photoshoot. Winnie saw Annie engage with her baby for the first time since she'd been there. Annie had smiled and shown a sliver of her old energy.

"Mom, I can't live just for the small moments. That's not enough for me. I can't stand this feeling and knowing that I have to feel it every day."

"You won't," Winnie said, and she sure hoped it was true.

Annie

She could feel Susan's eyes on her pile of medications. It had increased to more than just Lithium, Paxil, Trazadone, and Xanax. Dr. Ruman had called her every day after their visit, and when she wasn't feeling significantly better, he had her come in after forty-eight hours of trying the medications. He added a low dose of Abilify and a low dose of Klonopin to help her sleep better. Annie hadn't taken the Xanax. She already felt ashamed about how many medications she was taking to barely function. She didn't want Susan to see her like this.

Susan didn't really know Annie. When they were together, Annie typically let her do the talking, and Susan liked to talk. If there was a lull, she would ask questions about Michael as a kid. She usually enjoyed hearing the stories that Susan had to tell, but now she didn't have the energy even to say "mmhmm" to Susan's stories. If Susan brought up politics, she was pretty sure she'd fall apart.

Annie was embarrassed for Susan to see her with Avery. It wasn't natural anymore like it had been when she was still breastfeeding Avery. Normally, Annie would sing and talk to Avery while changing a diaper, she would lay next to her on the floor while she practiced tummy time, she would read her black and white books, and she would snuggle her close, kissing her soft, squishy cheeks.

She was also always on top of taking care of Nicholas. His routine was very structured, and he was her buddy. He went to her with every cut or scrape to kiss, when he had a question about the way something worked, or when he needed someone to find a toy that he couldn't find that was sitting right in front of him. Now, she couldn't do any of this. She really tried her best with Nicholas because she so greatly feared he would notice a difference, but she couldn't bring herself to even sing a song to Avery. If she tried, she knew she'd break down into tears. She worried that just by holding Avery, she would somehow transfer what she was feeling to the precious baby and ruin her for the rest of her life.

Susan went straight for the kids. Whenever she came to visit, she came with a bag full of treats and surprises for Nicholas. Annie was relieved for Nicholas to be distracted, and Susan couldn't get enough of Avery. She would spend hours just lying on the floor watching her wiggle her little legs in the air trying to work out gas. Michael was still home the first day, so Annie felt like she was free for the first time since Avery was born, and this made her feel a sense of relief she hadn't felt in weeks. She allowed herself to take a nap in the afternoon, and although she was quite dazed from all of the medication, she did feel a bit better.

When Michael went back to work, Susan started making her cooking plans. Annie wasn't picky, and knew whatever Susan cooked would be delicious. She still didn't have much of an appetite and had been living off of Pedialyte, Gatorade, and ginger ale, so she wasn't sure she'd be able to eat what Susan cooked anyhow. She was, however, glad to not have to worry about meals for Michael and the kids for a few days.

Susan needed to go to the grocery store, so Annie told her she could take her car. Annie should have known that Susan would scoff at such a remark. She didn't drive either. One of the main reasons someone needed to be with Annie is because she couldn't drive, yet the person who had come to help didn't either. Susan always let her husband drive everywhere. They only had one car in Florida, and although Susan had her license, she never took it anywhere herself. She looked to Annie to take her. This also meant that they had to bring Avery, which was an ordeal at that age.

Annie struggled to think about what to make sure she had in the diaper bag. She knew she needed a bottle to prepare just in case, diapers, a change of clothes, and wipes. She knew it was just the grocery store, but had also learned with Nicholas that anything could happen. Her worst memory of being unprepared was when she had been to the grocery store with Nicholas as a newborn, and when she came out to the car, her battery had died. Luckily, she was still breastfeeding at the time, or they would have been stranded in the parking lot, Nicholas screaming for food. Either way, she never left home without everything one could need in case of an emergency.

This was the opposite of what Annie was supposed to be doing. She was supposed to be taking care of herself, and she didn't even want to eat a thing. However, Susan wouldn't feed her son a grilled cheese sandwich and soup for dinner like Annie would have preferred, so off to the grocery store they went. While they were at the store, Susan kept asking her questions about what she wanted to eat. She may have been asking her other questions as well, Annie wasn't sure. She was overstimulated by the grocery store, overwhelmed with the decisions that she'd have to make, even though it was just about what to eat. She hadn't made a list, and there were probably items that they needed in the house, but Annie couldn't think of them. She stared at the cereal aisle knowing Nicholas probably needed a box, but was paralyzed by how many options there were to choose from. Even if she picked the type, there were different flavors and sizes. She didn't remember the grocery store requiring so many decisions.

Susan was throwing all kinds of items in the cart that Annie knew she wouldn't be able to stomach, like a large squash, Mexican seasoning, and chicken, but she didn't protest. She just pushed Avery around in the stroller following Susan around staying quiet. On the way home, Susan began talking politics in the car. "Did you know that Democrats believe in full-term abortions? That they think it's okay to kill a baby even at forty weeks?"

Even in her catatonic state, and as she tried to keep her focus on driving, Annie couldn't help herself. "Susan, that's not true. I'd love to see your source."

"Oh, I'll show you when we get home, you'll see. It's despicable."

"It is despicable and also untrue."

"No, Annie, you'll see." Annie was losing energy fast. She needed to get home and put herself to bed.

When she got home, as they were putting away the groceries, Susan noticed they had forgotten to bring home lettuce even though apparently Susan had discussed with her that they needed it. "Can you believe we both forgot?" Susan laughed, "I just can't believe after discussing it, we went home without it!"

Annie had no recollection of them discussing the need for lettuce. She hadn't forgotten; she just hadn't heard a word Susan had said. Before they finished putting away the groceries, Susan was on her phone pulling up the abortion article. It turned out, she hadn't quite read through the article thoroughly, and Annie had been correct. She couldn't help but feel a little smug, but what she really needed to do was lie down. She reviewed Avery's schedule with Susan, and went up to bed.

When she awoke, she decided to take a shower because she could feel the familiar feeling of bugs crawling over her body. She had learned that showering really calmed the feeling. There were some days where she was showering two or three times a day when Michael had been home. Annie walked down the stairs to Susan giving Avery a bottle an hour earlier than she was supposed to. "She never slept. I thought you said she would sleep. I think she's hungry."

Annie could see Avery falling asleep at the bottle. She was clearly overtired, but Annie was so thankful for the break that she didn't say anything to Susan. Normally, the children getting off schedule would cause her great anxiety. In fact, normally, she wouldn't be able to leave the children unattended with Susan. It wasn't that Susan couldn't be trusted to care for her children; Annie was just so particular that it was hard for her to let go. Only her own mother had Annie's motherly instincts, and did everything exactly as Annie did, or maybe Annie learned it from her own mother first. She thought to herself that the medicine must be working because she was letting it go as quickly as it came.

As to be expected, Susan made a gourmet meal for dinner. Annie found herself wanting to hold Avery for the first time in days, just lying on the couch waiting for Nicholas to come home. She stared at her daughter with adoration instead of fear. Her insides weren't in knots as she laid on the coach letting Avery sleep on her chest. It was the first day she didn't have a sense of dread for when Michael would be bringing Nicholas home. It wasn't that she didn't want to see Nicholas. She loved her son. She just didn't have the energy to cover up what she had been feeling, and dreaded having to muster it up for his arrival. This time, she was looking forward to hearing about Nicholas's day.

Annie found herself eating what Susan had cooked because it was just so delicious. She had made a butternut squash soup, chicken piccata meatballs, and a rice dish full of delicious spices. In fact, Annie even helped herself to second helpings. "It's so nice to actually see you eat something, Ann," Michael commented.

Annie laid on the couch watching her mother-in-law play with her kids. It felt like it had been so long since she had sat and played with Nicholas and was glad that there was someone to do that with him. She was always so busy with the baby, and Michael always had so much paperwork when he came home, that Nicholas tended to be left to his own devices more often since Avery had been born. Annie felt a rumbling in her stomach like she was going to be sick, but tried to ignore it. Her body actually felt relaxed lying there, until the cramping in her abdomen became much worse.

Annie darted from the couch to the bathroom where she had explosive diarrhea that just seemed to keep coming. Apparently, she shouldn't have had the second helping at dinner. This continued to happen after every meal during her mother-in-law's visit until it had been six days and she was able to stop the Lithium. Dr. Ruman just wanted to break the cycle, and after continuing to check in with her by phone each day, it was clear she was drastically improving. He told her she could wean off of the Lithium over a few days, and Annie was relieved to be getting off of the drug. It had helped her, but her head didn't feel like her own, and it upset her stomach. Now that she was gaining back some of her energy, and felt comfortable in her own skin, she wanted to get back to the person she was before this all began. Annie wondered if any of her father's doctors called to check on him daily. Maybe if they had, they would know how much their recommendations and changes weren't helping.

Avery certainly tired out Susan. Annie stopped needing so many naps throughout the day and left Susan to take some while she took Avery for walks. She even walked her to a restaurant near the house and had a quiet lunch with her daughter alone. She knew that Susan was giving it her all during the visit. Normally, when she visited Susan in Florida, Susan took an afternoon nap every day. Susan didn't like to sleep in their guest room because it was on the basement floor. She referred to it as "the dungeon" even though Michael had spent weeks finishing it with new drywall, paint, and carpet. Winnie always slept there when she came to visit. Susan preferred the couch, so she probably wasn't getting the sleep she needed. She also put up with the local news instead of her beloved Fox News, which was on all day in her own home.

Susan really tried, and Annie felt that their relationship had improved from the visit. She still didn't feel like Susan really knew her, but it was clear that she accepted Annie for who she was and that she loved and supported her. Susan had dropped everything, leaving her husband for over a week to come to take care of Annie. It may not have been the exact way Annie wanted to be taken care of every minute, but she had certainly tried her best. Annie wasn't sure she would have been able to get back to herself without Susan, and for that, she was forever grateful.

Annie began getting back to exercising, inviting people for gatherings, and she even finally called Rye, apologizing for how distant she had been. She couldn't help but wonder if this was all her father needed, the right concoction of medication. It wasn't like he hadn't been to more doctors than she could count on two hands, and had tried more medications than she even knew existed, but it made her hopeful that her father could come out of it too.

When Susan left, Annie was relieved to get back to her old life again. She called Dr. Ruman her miracle worker when he called in to check on her. He was checking on her less frequently, and her appointments were becoming biweekly instead of multiple appointments per week. This was good because Annie was on extended maternity leave and couldn't really keep paying the three hundred dollars that she had to pay every time she visited Dr. Ruman. However, it was certainly worth it. She wished her father could find a Dr. Ruman.

Cade

"If he can't go to the after-school program without his aide, then you clearly haven't taught him anything. This is all news to me. I thought he was doing well. I thought that he had improved. You've been lying to me all this time." The parent was screaming at Cade. It was the second time she had been screamed at this week by a parent. In this week alone, Cade's entire life was falling apart, or at least that's how she felt.

A few days prior, she had gone to a meeting of a student who had been evaluated for special education. Since the special education teacher at the school was beyond useless, Cade had been responsible for sending home the rating scales to complete for the psychologist. Blue River didn't have a psychologist of their own, so if a student needed to be evaluated, they had to contract one out. The psychologist would come and meet with the student for the entire day, which for a student like Ramar wasn't the best practice. He could barely hold his attention for a ten-minute lesson, let alone spend his whole day being tested, but that's how it was done because the school couldn't afford to do it any other way.

Cade had been asked to fill out the rating scales herself, and the special education teacher had asked Cade to send home an envelope to the parent in the homework folder for the parent's input. The parent had never returned the rating scales, so when they got to the meeting, the only answers they reviewed were Cade's. The psychologist wasn't at the meeting because the school couldn't afford to pay him for that, so the person who was supposed to explain everything to the parent was the special education teacher. Cade should have known they were in trouble, but this was the first student who had ever been evaluated from her classroom.

The psychologist left recommendations that the report be shared with the pediatrician in order to discuss medication. He wrote that the parents never responded with the rating scales, so only Cade's answers were in the report. Cade didn't say anything because, from what she understood about the meeting, aside from how he did in class, there wasn't much else for her to say. She had already shared that at the beginning of the meeting as it was the reason for the referral in the first place.

Ramar's mother slammed her fists down on the table and got in Cade's face. "You want to put my child on medication!" she screamed at Cade. "Yeah, I didn't fill out those fucking papers you sent home. I couldn't read them!" Cade felt sorry for Ramar's mother. She thought about that as she filled out the rating scales. She knew that Ramar's mother hadn't graduated from high school because they had talked about it before at his parent conference. She also knew that Ramar's mother worked two minimum wage jobs for her and Ramar to live in their trailer. She didn't have time to be worrying about rating scales.

Ms. Jay inserted her body in between them and urged Ramar's mother to calm down. "Cade didn't make these recommendations, Ms. Simon. The psychologist did. We are sorry that you were unable to read the rating scales," she said as she gave a side glance to the special education teacher, who is supposed to help a parent if they can't read the rating scales on their own. She should have gone through them with Ms. Simon, reading them to her and making sure she understood how to respond to the questions, or the school should have a psychologist, since students were referred for special education services left and right at Blue River. Many of the students who came there had been having difficulty at the public schools due to a disability, and many were finally diagnosed once they got there. Fortunately, the teachers at Blue River had a great understanding of how to meet the needs of any student who came into their classrooms, so the children tended to succeed despite the lack of special education services there. "No one is telling you to put your child on medication either, Ms. Simon. It's just a recommendation from the psychologist that you share this with Ramar's pediatrician. It may be something to explore, but it is not anything you have to do."

Ms. Simon began to calm down and look apologetically at Cade. "Okay, I'm sorry," she directed to

Cade. "I just don't want my six-year-old on medication. He don't need that."

None of it was Cade's fault, but it had shaken her up. Even Ms. Jay had assured her she did nothing wrong because she saw that Cade was visibly upset after the meeting. She also heard Ms. Jay scold the special education teacher for not having done her job properly. Specifically, she yelled at her for putting her job all on Cade. It didn't make her feel any better, and she knew the whole process wouldn't change, that she would still be solely responsible for helping Ramar.

The week had also been the end of her and Ryan. In retrospect, she should have seen it coming, but she was still heartbroken. He was supposed to move there and start a life with her. She had believed, even though they had only known each other for a short while, that he was her forever. It became clear why he had become so distant on the phone. He was busy, but not with graduate school.

That night after the meeting, she called him hoping to receive some support after a hard day. "Cade, I can't talk about work right now. There's something I have to tell you." He had cut her off before she could even get into her story.

"Okay, what is it?"

"I don't know how to tell you this, but I'm seeing someone else."

It didn't register with her at first. "What do you mean you're seeing someone else?"

"I mean, I cheated on you. I need to end this relationship because I'm seeing someone else." Well, that was crystal clear.

Cade was so shocked that she didn't get angry. She didn't say anything at all except, "I have to go."

When they got off the phone, Cade just sat there staring off into space in her apartment, the apartment they were supposed to share together the following year. She looked out the window that overlooked a grassy hill and watched a moth flying through the sky. The moth flew in circles landing on pieces of grass in between. Her mind couldn't think about anything else except the life expectancy of moths. When she was younger, Winnie bought her a butterfly kit. The kit came with caterpillars that then formed a chrysalis and turned into butterflies all inside a net in their own house. When she and Winnie researched the butterflies, she learned that their life span in the wild was only two weeks. *How sad*, she had thought at the time, *for a creature to work so hard to come into the world only to live for two weeks.*

Cade had been the only one putting in the work for months into their relationship. She had been doing all of the calling, and when they did get on the phone, the conversation was strained, but she tried to keep it going. She felt like she should be more upset than she was. The shock wasn't really that the relationship had ended, but more that she had been so wrapped up in work that she didn't see the signs. They were all there loud and clear when she thought back over the past few months.

Now, three days after her berating during the meeting, and just one day after being dumped, she was being yelled at again, and this time it took her past her tipping point. There was only so much defeat she could take at one time. She had worked her tail off for Jimmy that year. He had come from a classroom just for students with autism to her general education classroom. His needs had been so severe in kindergarten, that the special education teacher created a room just for him. He spent most of his days in the special education trailer by himself with the aide to complete his work, joining the other students for specials, lunch, recess, and science or social studies.

When Cade arrived, she was floored by this. That was not inclusion. Cade created a behavior plan for him with a visual picture board rewarding him if he made it through small portions of the day. His rewards were timed with a visual timer she purchased with her own money to make sure that he could then transition to the next activity. She wore visual cards around her neck to remind him to keep his hands to himself, raise his hand before speaking, stay quiet while others spoke, and other expected behaviors of a first grader. During writing time, she got him to write about topics other than helicopters and the weather. He had become an integral member of the classroom, and now she was being told she did nothing for this child. He came to her only knowing his letters, unable to read a word, and was now reading only one quarter behind the rest of the class and only because he had so much difficulty understanding character perspectives. However, he was finally able to read and spell words.

Every single week, Cade sent home behavior report cards for every single student in the class. The guardians had to sign and return these, and she held on to every copy. She made comments, both positive and negative, when needed, for every student. Fridays weren't included unless a major event occurred, because this was how she spent Thursday afternoons, so they would be ready to go home in the Friday folders. She had been honest on Jimmy's papers. She would discuss his progress, but also his need for support throughout the day. Jimmy was now in the classroom, but he still required an aide. There were still times that he would get stuck, unable to move to the next activity, and Cade would need the help of the aide so she could move on with the rest of the class. During centers, Jimmy needed prompting to do his work and stay on task. Most importantly, eyes had to be on Jimmy at all times because he liked to hide behind bean bags or chairs and tickle the bottoms of the girls in class. He had made progress, but he couldn't be left to his own devices like the other students.

His mother had just opened her own business, and she needed him to go to the after-school program. The problem was that his aide ran the afterschool program, and felt another staff member would be necessary if he was going to attend. She already ran the program by herself and many of the students who attended were a handful. She knew, given the unstructured nature of the afternoons, he would have a very difficult time managing his behavior without someone with him one-on-one. His mother had just sent a note in his folder stating that he would be staying after school.

Cade immediately sent the teaching assistant to Ms. Jay with the note to be sure that this was okay, and as she expected, it wasn't. But Jimmy's mother couldn't have him running around her new store after school either. Cade and Ms. Jay understood that, and Cade agreed with Jimmy's mother that this went against the values of the school. They claimed to be inclusive, but were excluding him from something that was organized by the school. It didn't seem right, but the decision wasn't Cade's. Ms. Jay had been the one to deliver the message, but Jimmy's mother wasn't angry at Ms. Jay, she was angry at Cade.

Had Cade done enough for Jimmy? She wished that she had been able to get him to a point where he didn't need an aide anymore. His progress had been astounding, but she understood that he wasn't like the rest of the children. In fact, there had been parent complaints about him to her on field trips and during class events.

Sometimes those kinds of situations made him so overstimulated he had to take a break away from the other students with his aide. She had included him to the best of her ability, but now he was being excluded, and it didn't sit well with her.

The conversation was never really resolved, and Cade, inappropriately, ended up walking Jimmy to his mother's store down the road because she couldn't come to pick him up at school. She said she would need someone to bring him there, and Cade felt like she needed to talk to his mother again after their phone conversation, so she took him there. The store seemed to be full of junk, but was advertised as a gift store. When she came in, Jimmy's mother was organizing a shelf of snow globes with no specific theme. It wasn't like people were coming to collect snow globes of their small town. There was one with Mickey Mouse, one with Santa Claus, one with a woman pulling baked bread out of the oven, snow globes of all walks of life. When she saw Jimmy and Cade walk in, she sighed.

"I know that he can't be left alone. It's just so hard. I don't know how I'm supposed to move forward with my life."

Cade couldn't fully understand because she didn't yet have children of her own, but she felt for Jimmy's mother. How hard it must be to not know if and when your child would ever be independent. "I'm sorry that he couldn't go to the after-school program."

"I know it's not your fault. I know that he's made strides this year. Hell, two years ago he was sitting in a room with eight other children all with autism. He couldn't even have a conversation with another child."

"He has made a lot of progress this year, but we should have a way for him to go to the after-school program like everyone else."

"I knew when I brought him to Blue River that the funding would be lower. There would be fewer resources even though he would be more included. It was the tradeoff I agreed to."

Cade simply nodded, and backed out of the store. Walking back to the school, the defeat turning into deep self-pity. She wasn't going to stay after school two hours that night. She couldn't. She needed to drive herself home, pour a big glass of wine, and have a good cry on her couch. If she didn't have the prospect of Ryan coming to join her, she was not as stuck in North Carolina as she had been before. If her job was taking all she had to give, maybe it was no longer the right place for her. Maybe part of her problem was that she felt stuck, and she needed to cut the cord.

Winnie

The thud sounded like a tree had fallen inside her living room, jolting her awake. She bolted down the stairs without looking to see the time. It was still dark out, and Winnie had been fast asleep. She knew it was Don before she entered the living room. Her couches made an L-shape facing the television in the opposite corner. Don was lying on the floor, his head in the corner of the two couches, his legs by the dividing wall between the living room and the kitchen. There was an opening in the wall, and Don's medications were set on the counter. The medication holder hadn't been opened yet with Monday morning's medication. Winnie didn't know what happened, but Don wasn't moving.

Gordina had come running out too. "Oh ma'am, what has happened?"

"I don't know." She looked at the clock. It was just a little after four in the morning. It wasn't completely rare for Don to be up at this hour. Because he always laid in bed, morning for him was sometimes at this time. She frequently heard him getting himself breakfast, or Gordina making him something to eat, and would look at her clock to see it was only just four or five in the morning. When he woke up, he would walk to that area of the living room to get his medication. Winnie set it out for him each week, so he knew which pills to take and when.

Gordina got to the floor, Winnie was too stunned to move. "He's still breathing ma'am. You need to call 9-1-1."

Winnie got out her phone and dialed. "Yes, hi. My husband is on the floor. No, I don't know what happened. He's not moving. Yes, he's still breathing. No, he's not conscious." She gave her address and hung up the phone. "They're on their way," she said to no one in particular.

Just then she looked down and saw Don trying to speak. "Winnie...Winnie. I fell. I...I...don't..."

"Shh," she told him. "Just relax. Help will be here soon."

"I fell. My ribs. My hip. My head. I think I broke..." Don didn't finish.

Gordina just kept apologizing. "I'm so sorry, ma'am. He always wakes me up if he wants breakfast. I was asleep. I didn't hear him get up. I'm so sorry. It's my fault. I'm sorry."

"It's not your fault," Winnie assured Gordina. Although, she wondered if Don had done something stupid again while Gordina was sleeping. Did he sneak medicine? Would she find cuts somewhere? What had caused him to be lying on the floor?

When the paramedics arrived, they took his vitals. His blood pressure was extremely low. They concluded that it was likely that he had fainted from such low blood pressure. There was blood coming from Don's head that she hadn't noticed initially. As they tried to move him, he hollered in pain, clutching his ribs. He couldn't even sit up, let alone stand up on his own.

The paramedics got out a stretcher and hoisted him onto it. Don looked at Gordina and Winnie, scared as a puppy who is being taken away from its owner. Winnie told Gordina to stay home, but she got in the ambulance with Don. The whole way Don kept asking, "Winnie, what happened? What happened to me?"

"Are you sure he hasn't taken anything?" she asked the paramedics.

"We won't know until a blood screen has been done. We'll take good care of him. Don't worry."

When they arrived at the hospital, Winnie was sent to the waiting room. She looked down at her feet and realized she was still wearing her nightgown. On her feet were her flip flops, and she had only grabbed a sweater to wrap around herself. Suddenly embarrassed, she wished she could hurry back home and change her clothing. Then she felt ridiculous for even worrying about such a thing. Who cared what she looked like when her husband was in this condition? The sun had come up, hours had passed, and Winnie still hadn't had her morning cup of coffee. Thankfully, she had grabbed her purse, so she walked to the cafeteria to get herself a cup.

This feeling was all too familiar for Winnie. She thought back to all of the times she had rushed to the hospital with Don and the many cups of hospital coffee she had in different waiting rooms. This time, the doctors who took Don from her had been friendlier, more reassuring. It wasn't like when he was brought to the psychiatric or detox units. There, they had been treated as inferior. The doctors didn't feel the need to keep her informed. There was no reassurance that anything would be okay. They looked at her and her husband as another problem the system had to tackle.

As she waited, sipping her coffee, the doctor came out to meet with her. "Mrs. Sanders?"

"How's he doing? What even happened?"

"Mrs. Sanders, your husband has taken a serious fall. He has a head injury. He has numerous fractured ribs on both sides and several pelvic fractures. One of his ribs has punctured his lung. We need to do an emergency procedure to relieve the fluid in his lungs. Come with me so you can see Don and sign the release to do the procedure. I'm so sorry."

Winnie almost cried with gratitude. It was the first time she had heard those words from any of the medical professionals she had encountered. *I'm sorry*. It was the first time anyone had acknowledged that this might be difficult for her and not just for Don. When he went to the detox center, she felt that the doctors believed it was her fault. That she had somehow enabled this behavior in her husband, which maybe to an extent she had given the many years he abused the drugs, but never once did they recognize that this was also difficult for her. After the first suicide attempt, when he ended up in the ICU with liver damage, it was hours before anyone even acknowledged her presence. When they did, she felt like they believed it was her fault that he had taken the Tylenol in the first place. They questioned her about why he did it, like anyone could fully understand why someone else would try to take their own life. It was like she should know, and part of her felt like they believed she was responsible for it. When Don drove himself into a lake, the police had been serious, not rude, but didn't offer comfort in any way. When she went to the hospital, yet again, she was so concerned about where he was going to end up next, and she had been so harsh with the employees who didn't have answers that they had ignored her when they could, and answered her with a similar attitude in return when they tried to give her recommendations.

His last hospital visit, when he tied the elastic from his clothes around his neck, she was sure the people at Willows had told them how crazy she was. No one listened to her. No one wanted to hear the full story. It was just more medication changes despite Winnie trying to explain all that had been tried. Just those simple words—*I'm sorry*—almost brought her to her knees.

She went in to see Don. She was glad the doctor had warned her what to expect. They were stitching up a gash on his head and his breathing was labored, and as he tried to talk, she put her finger to her lips knowing that he shouldn't be trying to talk to her. There was nothing to say. It was the first time he didn't need to be apologizing. He hadn't done anything wrong. This wasn't his fault. Why his blood pressure was so low had been an ongoing mystery, just like the rest of his illness.

A kind doctor gave her a form to sign to allow the necessary procedure to help his breathing by inserting a tube to drain the fluid in his lungs. He even offered her a chair as it was clear she was overwhelmed. Winnie began to explain that though this was necessary, they needed to include her in discussions about care going forward. She tried to tell him that this was part of a long battle with Don's continued decline and increasingly poor quality of life. She wondered to herself what this all meant. Was this what would finally get Don what he had hoped for every day, an end to his suffering? Would it end this nightmare or just bring a whole new tragic chapter to an unbelievable story? What she did know was that she would continue to advocate strongly for what she knew to be Don's wishes. They had discussed these many, many times in their lives and had promised each other they would speak for each other when it was needed. He had clear advanced directives with a living will and a MOLST form with doctor's orders for a DNR and DNI.

This had been initiated by Don himself much earlier when he felt himself changing and feared he would lose the capacity to make his own decisions. It had recently been reviewed and renewed by his primary physician. If treating these numerous problems would only result in pain, poor quality of life, and living in a nursing home, Winnie was not passively going to allow this to happen.

Winnie knew what the outcome was going to be for Don. He wasn't going to simply recover from this. Don was already living his worst nightmare. Cognitively, he was no longer functioning like himself. He lived in a world of delusion and obsessive thoughts. Physically, he was already in a deteriorated state. Any sort of intervention would require months of rehabilitation only for Don to end up in a nursing home. He couldn't come home after this. Even with around-the-clock care, this was how Don had ended up. He wasn't safe or fit to live at home, and Winnie knew he was never coming home again.

The doctors were there discussing the plan. Don's speech began to slur, and an emergency X-Ray showed a worsening brain bleed. They were preparing to bring him to the Neuro ICU where they might need to do a surgical procedure on his brain. He was also having continued difficulty breathing that they thought would also require intensive care.

"No!" They stopped mid-sentence, turning to face Winnie. "He has a DNR and a DNI and clear advanced directives. He's not going to any ICU, and there will be no surgery."

"But Mrs. Sanders," they explained, "if we don't intervene, the brain bleed might get worse and he might get pneumonia."

The doctors looked at her like she was heartless, like she wanted her husband to die. "He's right there. Why don't you let him tell you?" Winnie said.

"Dr. Sanders, we want to take you to the ICU to deal with your labored breathing and brain bleed. If we don't start this type of treatment it is likely your situation will become worse. Do we have your permission to intervene?"

Don shook his head. "No," he mouthed, but little came out.

"Do you understand, Dr. Sanders, that if we don't intervene, it is unlikely that you will recover on your own?"

"Yes," Don mouthed.

"Don, all you want are measures that will make you more comfortable. Isn't that right?" Winnie knew Don couldn't say this himself.

Don nodded his head. The doctors looked at one another. Winnie knew that this went against what they were trained to do. She had been a social worker for Hospice the majority of her career. It had been her job to help people carry out these wishes, to help them receive comfort measures only. She had advocated for families many times, discussing with doctors about what the patients wanted and clarifying the goals of care. Now it was very clear to her what the goals of care were for Don. She would not allow him to suffer in pain while they futilely tried to salvage life that would result in endless ongoing suffering for Don.

There were two different schools of thought. Doctors were trained to fix problems, to save lives. They were meant to intervene when there was a problem and do anything possible to keep a person alive. It was not their job to decide for a patient whether the quality of life they would have in the end would be worth it. Every life was worth it. Winnie felt differently and knew that Don shared her feelings as well. In the end, Don would be living in a nursing home, and who knew whether he would ever be walking again, or if he even wanted to.

Winnie didn't know how the process would unfold, but she knew that this was going to be it for Don. After all the times he tried to end his own life, the saga was going to come to an end, just not on his own terms. This time, it was in God's hands. Winnie didn't know why his blood pressure had dropped as low as it had, but she knew all along that there was something terribly wrong with Don. She didn't know if it was in relation to all the medications he took for his mental illness, spreading of his prostate cancer, early-onset dementia, or one of the many diseases she had researched over the past two years that fit any of his symptoms, but now the illness had caused him to have a fall, and this fall was going to be the end for him. She had to call the girls. She didn't know how much time Don had left.

Rye

The parent said it was an emergency, that it was absolutely imperative that Rye call her as soon as she had a moment. When Rye saw the email, she immediately went looking for the psychologist, but she couldn't find her. Max had a history of being suicidal. She didn't know if they were going to have to spend their afternoon calling 2-1-1. In the email, his mother had written that he had made alarming comments to her at home. Did he have a plan? She only saw him three days per week, and today wasn't one of those days. She ran to see him in class, and he was sitting in English, doing his work like everyone else. Rye didn't want to disrupt him before knowing what the problem was.

She went back to her office and called his mother. "Hi Mrs. Miller, I just saw your email."

"Oh yes, Rye, thank you for calling me back. We need to talk."

"Yes, I saw it was an emergency. What's going on? Do I need to get Dr. Pinket too?"

"Oh, I don't think that will be necessary."

"Okay, well what's the problem. What is Max saying at home?"

"He's bored in science." It was rare that Rye lost her patience with a parent. She received all kinds of "emergency" phone calls. She had received an email from a parent to call her that night if she had a moment because a teacher had made a mistake on the answer key he posted online for the students to look at to check their homework. A parent had emailed her on the weekend because she was sure Rye didn't send home a modified study guide, and there was absolutely no way her son was going to be ready for the test at the end of the week, to which Rye sent again the email she had sent just the day before with the modified study guide. Rye was used to the fact that parents in the district took school very seriously. She knew that many of the mothers didn't work, and would call or email her about their child's grade the minute it was posted online before she had even seen it. But this? This pushed her beyond her limit. There she was having panicked and raced through the building thinking she was dealing with a situation that teetered on life or death, and a child was simply bored in class. It was seventh grade. Welcome to the club.

Rye tried to stay patient. "I see, and what makes this an emergency exactly?"

"Well, last year when he became bored in his classes was when everything spiraled."

Rye began to feel empathy for this woman who had seen her son want to end his own life. She couldn't imagine watching either of her girls feel so depressed they didn't want to live anymore. She would be on guard if any of the same behaviors from the time reappeared again too. However, she wasn't too sure, as the special education teacher, what she could do to make a child more interested in a class that she didn't teach.

"Have you talked to the teacher, Mrs. Smith?"

"No, I'm talking to you." Mrs. Smith could be very intense, but Rye was used to this. At first she found it off-putting, but they had developed a relationship at this point in the year, so Rye could be just as blunt.

"Mrs. Smith, you need to talk to the science teacher. As much as I'd like to, I can't change how another teacher teaches their class."

"No, but you can tell him how Max is bored, and how when this has happened in the past, it has caused him to completely check out from school. And when he completely checks out of school, he becomes depressed and hopeless."

"Mrs. Smith, I have discussed Max at all of our weekly team meetings, and he is well aware of Max's history. I will certainly discuss it again, but I still think it's best that you talk to the science teacher about his class."

"You're right." When you stood up to Mrs. Smith, she always backed down. She respected it. "I'm sorry for bothering you about this."

"You're never bothering me," Rye lied. "We will keep our eye on Max. We are not going to let him check out of school completely. It's good to keep us informed. Thanks for letting us know. Just, in the future…my mind went elsewhere when you said it was an emergency, so maybe you can let me know a bit more information in the email, so I have an idea of what we will be discussing."

"I'll do that. Thank you Mrs. Hue."

Rye hung up the phone and saw a missed call from her mom. There was also a text message: "call when you can." Winnie didn't leave messages like that unless there was a problem. She closed her classroom door and dialed Winnie's number. She had a feeling that in a moment she would be dealing with a true emergency.

"Where are you right now?" Winnie asked.

"I'm in my classroom. What's going on, Mom?"

"Are you by yourself?"

"Of course. I wouldn't call after seeing that kind of text message with students in the room."

"Your father has had a fall."

"What? What kind of fall?"

"I don't really know what happened, Rye. I found him on the floor at four this morning." Rye looked at the clock. It was almost the end of the school day.

"Mom, why didn't you call me sooner?"

"Rye, I'm sitting here still in my nightgown. I haven't eaten anything all day. I didn't have a chance. The doctors aren't listening to me again…"

Rye cut off her mother. "What do you mean they aren't listening to you? What do you have to tell them about? Was this from another suicide attempt?"

"No, No. Actually, I really don't know why he fell. The doctors think that he passed out from his blood pressure being so low. You know how he's had blood pressure issues. It was even lower than it had been when the doctors had been concerned in the past."

"What did he hurt? Is something broken?"

"Oh honey, it's much worse than that."

"What do you mean?"

"He is bleeding from his brain, he's broken multiple ribs, he has several pelvic fractures and he punctured a lung. He's in critical condition. That's what I mean about the doctors not listening to me. They keep trying to do interventions that go against your father's wishes. He is never coming back from this. He's never coming back from this."

"How do you know, Mom? Why wouldn't you let the doctors help him?"

"Rye, even if they can get control of the bleeding in his brain, which could require surgery, and somehow his lungs improve, he may never regain any mobility, and he will have problem after problem. He will have to go through months of rehabilitation. He will end up in a nursing home. It would be his worst nightmare, worse than the one he's already been living."

"I'm coming there right now." Rye had hung up before her mother could protest.

Rye was friends with her boss, and her boss knew that there had been issues going on with her father for the past two years. Rye told her it was an emergency, and she had to leave. She left all of her work at school knowing that she wasn't going to be looking at it that night and rushed to the hospital.

As Rye pulled into the parking lot, she had the familiar feeling she recognized from meeting her mother there other times her father was in crisis. She always took a deep breath in the car, reminding herself to stay calm and patient. She knew her mother would be hyper and yelling at the doctors, embarrassing her and making it so Rye couldn't ask any of her own questions. She got out of her car and walked down the stairs to the entryway of the hospital. The staff at the front desk were always friendly when she walked in. She almost wished they weren't because she didn't feel like smiling back. They pointed her in the direction of her father's room

When she walked in, her father was lying with his eyes closed. She felt deep sympathy for him. He looked so pathetic lying there, and he didn't look like the man she had seen just days ago playing ball with her daughters. His head was bandaged where he had a large gash. His breathing was labored and she could hear him wheezing as he took in each breath. As she stepped in closer, her father's eyes opened, closed, and then opened sharply, clearly surprised to see her there.

"Hi, Dad."

Don tried to talk, but all that came out was a whisper. "Rye, what are you doing here?" He then began coughing and clutching his ribs, moaning. It was painful for Rye to see. She just wanted his pain to go away. Winnie jumped up and said she was going to find a nurse to get him more pain medicine. She was clearly overwhelmed as she rushed around in her nightgown.

"All I asked is that they fucking keep him comfortable. No one listens to me," Winnie muttered to herself as she flew out the door.

"Your mother…" Don trailed off.

"It's okay, Dad. Don't try to talk."

"Rye, I'm so sorry."

"There's nothing to be sorry for, and you really don't look like you should be talking."

"I wish I had been a better father." Don was coughing and continuing to groan. Rye couldn't keep watching him in so much pain. She was relieved when she saw her mother come back with a nurse in tow.

"Dr. Sanders, we are going to give you some morphine, okay? You are going to feel less pain."

"How is he doing?" Rye asked the nurse.

"He has numerous problems that may get worse, but we're trying to keep him as comfortable as we can as we develop his care plan."

"And no one will listen to me that he doesn't want aggressive intervention," Winnie chimed in angrily.

"Mom, please. Let her talk."

"If there are no interventions, it is likely that Dr. Sanders is going to get pneumonia. It's going to get progressively harder for him to breathe."

"He just wants to be comfortable," said Winnie.

"Dad," Rye asked, "is that really what you want? To just die?"

Don nodded his head and then looked away, unable to hold eye contact with Rye. Rye felt her eyes fill with tears. She didn't like to cry in front of anyone. She stepped out and heard her mother follow after her. She turned around holding up her hand. "Mom, please. Just let me be."

Rye didn't want the doctors and nurses rushing by to see her either. She walked to the waiting room, but there was a family sitting there. Through blurry eyes, she asked where the bathroom was, and the family directed her. She ran inside of a stall and just stared down at the toilet, letting the tears finally fall from her eyes. A few of the tears dripped into the toilet, and Rye just stared watching the water ripple into circles. She knew it was what her father wanted. It was clear that he didn't want to live anymore as it was, but now that it was a real possibility, Rye wanted to do everything possible to keep him living. She knew she was being selfish, but she wanted her father to stay around for her, for her girls.

Rye pulled herself together and stepped out of the stall. She looked at herself in the mirror. It was obvious she had been crying, her eyes still wet with tears that were forming beyond her control. Her mother had clearly known she was upset, so she didn't know why she was trying to hide it, why she always tried to hide it. She hated to feel her mother's sympathy for her, and she hated for any of the situations with her father to be about her. Her mother would always ask if she was okay when they were in the hospital waiting room, in the cafeteria eating their first meal in twenty-four hours, or on the phone after they had both finally gone home. Of course, she wasn't okay, but she didn't know how to talk about it, not with her mother. Not even with Will. The only person she broke down in front of was her doctor when she went to get the Lexapro, and she was glad she wouldn't have to go back for another year.

Rye walked back into the room where her mother was finally talking calmly to the doctors. She knew her mother needed to go home, have a shower, change her clothes, and eat something. When her mother was done discussing Don's wishes and the plan to keep him comfortable with the doctors, Rye told her, "Mom, go home. I'll stay with Dad for a while. I can even stay until you want to come back."

"Oh sweetheart, I can't ask you to do that. It's okay. I'll be fine. You didn't even have to come here."

"No, Mom, I did have to come here, and so do Annie and Cade. We don't know how much longer Dad will be here."

"I can tell you from all my years in my job that we are in it for the long haul here. This is going to take time, but you're right. We need to tell Annie and Cade."

"Mom, you go home and tell them. I'll stay here until you come back."

Rye knew that Winnie was beyond exhausted because she agreed, and she would never have agreed to giving herself a break in her normal state. Winnie never wanted to put any burden on her daughters, just like Don. Rye sat next to her father, holding his hand. The morphine had kicked in and he was asleep, his breathing still labored, but he was no longer writhing in pain. Rye didn't know how she was going to do this—watch her father die.

.

Annie

The sun no longer made Annie feel guilty. When she was feeling her worst, she wanted it to be a gloomy, rainy day every day. She wanted to have an excuse for lying on her couch, staying inside all day. The sun made her feel worse. It was like Avery, another beautiful part of the world that she couldn't enjoy beckoning to her. She had felt like if the sun came out, it was purposely rubbing in her face the fact that she wasn't enjoying life. Now, Annie let the sun beat down on her face and she felt joy for the first time in weeks.

She was pushing Avery around in the stroller and enjoying a walk in the neighborhood. Annie had avoided the neighbors during what her psychiatrist referred to as her acute episode. She had quickly run in the house after doctor appointments before they could see her. Even when Susan was there and she began to go out for walks, she immediately called her mother, so that Winnie would be the only person she had to talk to. Now, she stopped and let them *ooh* and *aah* over Avery. She beamed as they told her how beautiful her baby was. Annie was taking time each morning to put Avery in cute outfits wearing headbands with bows attached. She wanted to show her off.

Her phone rang and she saw that it was Winnie.

"Perfect timing! I'm just out walking."

There was a pause on the phone before Winnie spoke. "Annie, I have to tell you something." Annie stopped in her tracks. Of course, just when she was feeling back to herself, her father had to go and do this again. Then her heart dropped. What if this time he had been successful? "What, Mom?"

"Your father has had a fall. I'm home now from the hospital. Rye is with him. I found him at four this morning after I heard a loud thud, and he was lying on the floor by my couches. The doctors aren't sure exactly what caused the fall, but he hit his head and is bleeding internally in his brain. He also cracked many of his ribs, one of which punctured his lung and he has several pelvic fractures. His breathing is very labored, and he's not doing well."

"Well, what are the doctors going to do for him?"

"They can do everything to keep him comfortable. He's not coming back from this. Your father has a DNR and DNI, and does not want any of the interventions he is being offered. He does not want to end up in a nursing home in worse condition than he was already in."

Annie tried to take this all in. A minute ago, she had been soaking up the sun, and now she was soaking in this new information. She already felt fragile, like she was just getting back to herself, but could still break easily. However, she was also still on so many different medications that she found herself unable to cry, though usually crying came easily to her.

"Annie, it's up to you, but I don't know how this is going to play out with your father. I think you might want to come here."

"Have you called Cade?"

"Not yet, I'm going to call her when we get off of the phone."

"I think Cade and I should come together. I'll talk to her after you do and set up a way for her to fly here first, and then I can pick her up at the airport and drive her to see Dad. Can we stay with you?"

"Of course, honey."

"Where's Gordina?" Annie didn't know why she asked this question, and realized it was stupid the moment it came out of her mouth.

"She's home. There's no reason for her to stay with me if Don is in the hospital."

"Right," Annie said, realizing she was worried about her mother being alone.

"Okay, well I'm going to call Cade now."

Annie knew that there would be a lot of logistics to figure out with Michael so that she could go see Don. He was going to have to watch both of the children, and he was going to have to take off time from work again. She texted him first, letting him know that her father was in the hospital once again. Then, she kept walking. She walked longer than she had since Avery had been born.

She was like a hamster in a cage, walking the same loops in her neighborhood over and over again.

She thought back to a winter when she was about ten years old. Her father had been in his home office all morning. He never used a real computer system, so she heard him dictating into his hand recorder and scribbling notes on paper. It was how he spent every weekend morning and most evenings when he came home after dinner. Annie didn't mind because she had a wild imagination as a child. The whole house was devoted to her many games of pretend. In the corner of the kitchen, a children's table was set up with two chairs and a legal pad. This was where she played therapist to her stuffed animals, or her family members if she could get anyone to sit there. If she got Winnie, Winnie would give her a quarter for her services. The basement was full of books she stamped as if she were a librarian, each inside cover filled with pink butterflies and blue flowers. She took worksheets out of the recycling bin at school and pretended to grade work after her stuffed animals completed it. This was another activity she tried to get Cade to do, but she didn't usually want to play because Annie was always the teacher. Winnie had a bin full of dress-up clothes, and Annie pretended she was a movie star, a famous singer, a dancer for the New York City Ballet. She put on performances for anyone who would watch that she had practiced for hours. The living room would be set up with stuffed animals sitting watching her as she organized a birthday party for her favorite one that day. Annie didn't have a problem keeping herself busy.

One weekend day in the winter, when Annie was ten years old, Don decided he wanted to take Annie sledding. They didn't do much together, not like him and Rye. Don only really liked to participate in athletic activities, and Annie wasn't very athletic. She was always a thin girl, and in her adult life she worked out, but as a child, she was never into sports. Annie didn't particularly want to go sledding. It would require her to put on her snowsuit and be out in the cold, neither of which she wanted to do. Plus, it was her teddy bear's birthday, and she had a party to plan.

Don said he would give her ten dollars if she went sledding with him. Annie didn't realize she was being bribed at the time, but this sounded like a pretty good deal. Her parents didn't give an allowance, so this was a lot of money she could save for the next time she went to the mall. There was a lot she could get at Claire's for ten dollars. She agreed to go sledding with Don at the local golf course.

Annie put on her snowsuit, hat, gloves, and boots, and Don packed the car with a sled they could both sit on. The hill at the golf course was larger than Annie remembered. She and Don hiked to the top. Out of breath, she sat in the sled with Don and rode down the hill. They did this over and over again, Annie having the time of her life. The rush when she flew down the hill felt like she was on a rollercoaster. Then, Annie started going by herself while Don sat in the snow and reveled in the joy of the day, spending time with his middle daughter alone, not something that occurred often.

Annie ran up the hill, got the sled ready, and went down the hill on the opposite side instead of the same trail she had been going down each time. There was a large hidden rock underneath the snow. Annie flew through the air and the sled landed on the ground, hard. Annie couldn't move, her back seized up from the fall. Don came running down the hill when he saw that Annie hadn't moved. Annie was crying hysterically on the sled saying that she couldn't move. Don carefully picked her up and carried her and the sled to the car. By the time they got to the car, Annie had calmed down and her back had relaxed, but she had injured it badly.

When they got home, Don told Winnie they needed to go to the hospital.

"The hospital!" Annie shrieked. "I'm not going. I'm not going. I'm fine. You can't take me there." She couldn't run away from her parents because she was having trouble walking. Winnie looked to Don for what to do. He was a medical professional, after all. The problem, though, was Don was a pushover and didn't want to upset his daughter. He didn't take her and let her spend the next two weeks picking items up off the floor by squatting straight down because she couldn't bend over. She had told him that she'd never go sledding with him again.

As Annie walked, she thought about this memory, and how she wished she hadn't told Don that they'd never go sledding again. He had felt so bad for what happened that he never asked her to go again. She never asked to go again either because Don went back to his weekends of working in his office, doing what he felt most confident doing.

She had hoped when she had children, especially when her father retired, that he would maybe be able to make up for some of the time he lost working and spend time with his grandchildren. He would get to experience the firsts that he missed with his own children. She had wanted him to take her children sledding in the winter, to have another chance at it. Annie noticed that Avery was awake in the stroller. It was time to feed her and figure out how to pack for saying good-bye to her father.

Cade

Cade enjoyed the car ride with Annie. It had been a long time since they talked so long together. She had been so wrapped in her own life in North Carolina, that she hadn't quite realized what Annie had gone through in the last few weeks. Winnie told her that Annie was having a hard time, but she didn't know the extent. Cade told Annie about Ryan and stories from her year that Annie appreciated because it had now been months since she'd been in the classroom. She was happy to be with her sister, but wished it was under better circumstances.

As usual, Cade was the last to hear about Don from her mother. She got more of her information from Annie, because by the time Winnie had called her, she was so exhausted from repeating the story that all she had really gathered was that Don had fallen and was dying. Her mother told her to just call Annie, so Annie filled her in and proposed the idea of them going together. Rye, apparently, was not going to go with them, as she had spent days by Don's side and she needed a break.

Cade had almost forgotten why she had flown to Annie's. She had let go of the sub plans she spent hours scrutinizing, feeling sorry for the substitute who would be in her classroom for the next few days. The days were hard enough for her, and she knew the children and exactly how her classroom was run each day. She had written them, her hands shaking, heart pounding, having difficulty concentrating on what the teacher would have the children working on each half-hour of the day. It was the first time her mind wasn't consumed by work, and she realized when it wasn't, she couldn't hold herself to the standard she had unknowingly set over the school year.

At the airport, she had watched all of the people sitting near her and walking by. She kept catching eyes with strangers and having to look away at her book she was pretending to read. Cade wondered what everyone's story was. Were they going on vacation somewhere tropical? Were they on their way home? Were they traveling for business? Were they also traveling because tragedy had hit their lives? She wouldn't know, just like they wouldn't know why she was getting on a plane. There she was staring at the pages of her book like a normal person, but she didn't feel like her usual self at all.

Cade felt nervous. She didn't know what she was going to say to her father. She loved him and had always felt loved by him, but the relationship had been somewhat strained. If he answered the phone when she called, back when he used to answer the phone, she would just ask, "Hi Dad, is Mom there?" She never had anything to discuss with her father. Growing up, she had been the last child left home when her siblings went off to college. By then, family dinner didn't exist anymore.

She ate dinner at the kitchen counter watching television, generally late, after she came home from dance.

He didn't know the names of her friends who came over regularly. While he went to all of her dance recitals and *Nutcracker* performances, he didn't know what part she had until he came to see. Winnie sewed the costumes and drove her back and forth to every rehearsal, and they talked about it regularly at home, but Don didn't know. They had stopped celebrating holidays together. Ever since Cade had stopped going to Hebrew school, she didn't celebrate Hanukkah with her father at home either. He lit the candles on the menorah and spoke the prayers to himself.

What was she going to say to her father? She wasn't angry at him for her childhood. He had done what he'd known how to do best—medicine. Without his hard work, Cade knew that her own life and that of her sisters would have been much different. They had every opportunity available and they all attended private colleges with no student loans. Her father had also put her through graduate school and helped her pay to live in an apartment there while she was student teaching and couldn't work. It was thanks to him that she was able to move to North Carolina before she officially started working. She wouldn't have even been able to go to the interview without his help to buy a plane ticket and rent a car. He had devoted his life to making sure his girls had whatever they needed, but as a father figure, he had been absent much of their lives, especially for Cade.

Annie and Cade arrived at Winnie's house in the middle of the afternoon. They exchanged quick greetings to one another, but Cade could tell that Winnie was itching to get back to the hospital. She had only left to shower, and Cade could tell that she hadn't slept much. Her mother was jittery and jumpy, so Annie offered to drive because neither of them felt comfortable getting in the car with her. To their surprise, Winnie accepted the ride.

The girls followed their mother into the hospital, down a long corridor, through a pair of double doors, and up two flights in the elevator. They followed her into the waiting room without realizing where they were going.

"I want to warn you that your father looks drastically different than the last time you saw him." Cade hadn't seen her father since she visited him at Willows, and she had never seen him looking worse. She couldn't imagine that he could possibly have deteriorated even more.

"Just let us see him, Mom," Annie said. She seemed more confident than Cade felt. Part of Cade wanted to stay in the waiting room. It was no wonder she was always the last to hear the family news; she felt useless in every situation. She had spent the year completely wrapped up in herself, thinking of her father only on the occasional drive. She was the baby of the family, and right now, she felt it was painfully obvious.

Winnie led them down the hallway to their father's room. He was sharing it with a boy her age. He had been in a serious motorcycle accident, and Cade could hear his family talking with him about possibly never walking again. She heard the boy sobbing along with his mother, both grieving life as they had known it. Cade wondered if her father was listening to this all day.

When she looked at her father, he seemed lifeless. He had tubes coming out in every direction, and his eyes were closed. Cade wanted to turn around and leave. They shouldn't be disturbing their father when he was trying to sleep. She felt out of place, like a nuisance, like she didn't have a right to be there after the way she had treated her father as a child.

"Shouldn't we let him sleep?" she whispered to her mother.

"He's not really asleep, Cade. He's just resting. He won't mind."

Don turned his head to face Cade and Annie ,who stood next to one another. Cade immediately felt her eyes fill with tears. Her father began talking fast with large gasping breaths as he spoke. "I can't believe you both came. I can't believe you came. You didn't have to come. You're both so beautiful, so beautiful. I can't believe you came. Annie, you just had a baby. Cade, you came all the way from North Carolina. You're so beautiful, both of you. I love you so much…" He would have kept going, but Winnie put her hand on his shoulder, signaling he should stop talking.

Annie spoke first. "Dad, of course we came. We love you. We love you so much." She sobbed as she spoke.

"Dad, we love you." It was all Cade could add. She couldn't find the words to say what she wanted to say. She didn't know what she wanted to say.

"I'm sorry. I'm sorry I wasn't a better parent."

"Dad, we don't even want to hear that," Annie said firmly. "You were a wonderful father."

"I wasn't there for you all like I should have been."

Annie continued to speak because Cade couldn't. "If we were in your position, would you want us to be spending our time telling you our regrets? We are here because we love you. We hold nothing against you. We feel nothing but love for you." It was true. Cade no longer held anything against her father. She had let go of any of her anger towards him long ago when she was in college. It was during this time that she began to see her father for who he was: a human being who was doing his best. He was best at his work, and she of all people could now understand what it was like for work to be all-consuming. Don had been an incredible doctor, and his success kept the family afloat. Without him, their lives would have looked completely different, and Cade knew this.

She finally spoke. "You were a father who loved unconditionally. I never once had to question whether you loved me. You were a wonderful doctor and beautiful human being. There was no way I wasn't going to come see you right now." She reached down and touched his arm.

The doctor came in while they were all there. Even though it was obvious he wasn't doing well, Annie asked, "How is he doing?"

"The tube we inserted in the emergency room continues to drain the fluid in his lungs, but he could still develop pneumonia. We are also concerned about his continuing brain bleed and, of course, all the fractures are causing pain. Dr. Sanders, I want to be sure we are doing what we can for you. We can still move you to the ICU and begin more aggressive care."

Winnie lost it. "No one is listening! His wishes are clear and documented. The other doctor talked about other comfort measures, and we've already agreed to all of those. Why is no one listening? I feel like I can't even leave, because if I do, you all will do whatever the hell you want without respecting his wishes."

Cade felt herself blush. She felt sorry for the doctor, who was just trying to do her job. Apparently, the day before, Winnie had come in as they were getting ready to wheel Don to the ICU to begin aggressive treatment. He had been so uncomfortable that he just gave in. Winnie stopped them and talked to her husband about his options because he hadn't been given them. She was upset with the doctors for not following his wishes, for trying to push him to accept care that went against his directives when there were other ways to help him with his pain. Aggressive treatment, Winnie pressed, was just going to lead to more pain, and a poor outcome. She kept reminding the doctors that Don was not in his right mind. He had been assessed by a neurologist over the past year who had deemed him competent to make his own decisions, but the entire family knew that Don's mind was impaired in many ways for reasons unknown.

Cade was still embarrassed by her mother's behavior, but the doctor seemed used to her by now. She asked to speak to the family out in the hallway. "Do you all understand that if you don't let us intervene, your husband," she looked at Winnie, "and father," looking at Annie and Cade, "is going to die?"

Winnie answered for them, "Yes, we know. These are his wishes."

Cade felt her eyes well up with tears for the first time since she had come to the hospital. Winnie walked over and put her arm around Cade.

They went back to the room. "It's comfort measures only, Dr. Sanders. Let me go get you some more pain medication. We can also do various things to help with your breathing."

"Thank you," her father replied breathlessly.

The respiratory therapist arrived with a breathing treatment that would continue, and they increased his pain medications, which they had been holding back on for fear it would interfere with his breathing. Most importantly, the tension in the room evaporated as a calm began to settle on everyone. It was only minutes until Don's eyes were beginning to close. The girls and their mother sat with him in silence.

Cade didn't know what the others were thinking about, but she was completely present in the moment. She realized that in many ways, she was extremely lucky. Many people who lose a loved one don't get a chance to say goodbye, and some people's last encounter causes great regret. Cade didn't know if this was truly the last time she would see her father, but if it was, her last words would have been reassuring him that she loved him. She forgave him, and wanted him to know this by telling him there was nothing that needed forgiveness. As Don began to truly fall asleep, she whimpered quietly, squeezing Annie's hand.

"Are you girls ready to go?" Winnie asked them. "It's okay if you'd like more time."

Annie answered for them. "Yes, let's let Dad sleep."

Cade didn't know if she was really ready to leave. She knew she would be flying back to North Carolina, and wouldn't be able to visit very easily again. It was likely that the next time she flew back to Connecticut would be for her father's funeral. She didn't know what standing in his room would do, but she was having difficulty leaving the room. Winnie and Annie started walking away, and

Cade allowed herself to follow. She gave one last look back at her father, silently wishing him peace.

Winnie

Doctors aren't trained to do nothing when they know a patient is sick and there are interventions that can be performed. Hospitals aren't designed to house people as they slowly die. Winnie understood that there would come a time when Don would have to be moved. She had worked with the hospital social worker to find a Hospice care facility nearby. This was Winnie's element. She had worked in Hospice care homes her entire career. She had helped families with end-of-life care.

None of Winnie's experiences prepared her for watching her daughters have to say good-bye to their father. While she felt relieved that Annie was much less fragile than she had been, she worried that this would set her back. She was worried about Annie, but she was most concerned about Cade. Winnie knew that Cade had always had a strained relationship with Don. It had always been difficult for her to decide whether or not to intervene. She had always stayed out of it, but maybe she should have pushed Cade harder. Maybe she should have forced her to finish Hebrew School. Maybe she should have kept family dinners going even when Annie and Rye had gone to college and Cade was the only daughter left in the house.

Rye had been coming to visit Don at the hospital after work every single day. Winnie generally used this as her time to go home and take a shower. That was part of the reason she left. She also couldn't bear to watch Rye, the closest to her father, see him in this state. When he breathed, the fluid moving in his chest could be heard as a broken gurgle. He continued to do the breathing treatments, but they didn't seem to be making a difference. He couldn't move on his own, so the nurses regularly came in to turn and position him. The nurses were caring, kind, and professional, always asking if the family needed anything. Most of the time, Don was asleep from all of the morphine he was receiving. It was actually the calmest he had been in a long time.

The hospital was going to put Don in an ambulance and transport him to the Hospice facility that afternoon. Winnie was waiting, antsy to get Don settled in the new facility. She sat by his bed, perking up whenever a nurse or doctor came in. Finally, a nurse came in to wheel him down to the ambulance. It was the first time Don would be transported in an ambulance that Winnie didn't have to go inside. She wouldn't have to sit awkwardly with the medical professional making small talk. Winnie would meet them there in her own car.

Winnie found herself thinking about when the kids were young and the family went to Mexico. She got food poisoning so severe she had told the family "to leave her there to die." All she could do was lay in bed as she looked out the window of the hotel that overlooked the beach she couldn't enjoy. Annie spent most of her time in the hotel with her mother. She had brought along her Polly Pockets, and all she wanted to do was stay in the hotel room and play with them or watch television. Cade was the only one who wanted to go swimming in the water, but she couldn't because she had gotten a terrible case of impetigo. Fortunately, Don had been able to get the antibiotic ointment at a local pharmacy, but Cade couldn't put sunscreen on her face without screaming. She spent most of the vacation watching television with Annie.

Rye was a teenager at the time, and although not an incredibly difficult one, still wanted nothing to do with the family. There was an arcade down the street from the hotel, and Rye enjoyed the freedom of being able to walk there alone. It was all she wanted to do besides make fun of Cade for being a "leper." Cade didn't know what that meant, but it sent her running to Winnie in tears. Winnie had been too weak to yell at Rye and couldn't get out of bed to find Don to handle them, not that he would have known how to anyway.

Don spent the vacation the way he spent most of their family vacations—enjoying himself alone. He ran on the beach in the mornings, and he went swimming in the ocean by himself in the afternoon. He was so used to not having to be the caretaker of the children that he didn't know how to take the lead when Winnie was sick.

So, the vacation consisted of Winnie sick in bed in the hotel, Annie off in her imaginary world as usual, Rye testing her independence at the arcade, Cade whining about the scabs all over her face, and Don living the bachelor life in Mexico. In Winnie's eyes, the vacation had been a disaster for everyone except Don.

Winnie had walked to the parking lot of that hospital so many times. There were so many instances she had parked her car there thinking that it would be her last day with Don. When he was in the ICU and when he had given himself two strokes, she had grieved the loss of her husband long ago. Now, it was time to end his life peacefully and painlessly. He had been trying to end his pain himself all of this time, and now he would experience relief. That's what Winnie hoped death was for him. She hoped that it would be like their trip to Mexico. Don enjoying himself vacationing alone.

Rye

The nachos kept coming. Rye didn't know how many more salty, cheesy, crispy chips she could fit in her stomach. They had already ordered hot dogs, and she knew her father was going to finish off with ice cream. Every time the Red Sox hit a home run, her father got up out of his seat, throwing his fist into the air cheering. His excitement was infectious, and Rye would start jumping up and down joining him. Don loved the Red Sox like they were another family member. Every birthday, Winnie would buy Don Red Sox paraphernalia—a hat, a t-shirt, a book about the players. He had grown up in Boston and gone to Harvard, and the Red Sox had always been an integral part of his life.

Don would spend endless money on the food, but refused to spend a dime on parking. Rye always left the games tired, her stomach hurting, thinking she wasn't going to make the walk back to the car. On the way there, it was always easier because Rye was so excited to see the game, but leaving, the walk always felt significantly longer. Once, Rye even threw up on the walk home from all they had eaten. Don told her not to tell Winnie because he knew that she would yell at him for feeding Rye so much food.

As Rye got older, she began having beers with her father at the games. He still gave her the play by play about what was happening on the field even though she already knew the ins and outs of the game. She was pretty sure her father knew that she knew too, but it made him feel good to explain it to her. In between innings, her father liked to walk around the stadium, walking near the dugout to watch the players warm-up. Her father would call out encouragement to the players, which always made Rye slightly embarrassed, but she cherished going to the games with her father.

Rye had always shared her father's love of sports. As a kid, she had played softball and basketball, her father coaching both. She always felt guilty that her father never got involved with any of her sisters' activities, but he didn't know how to engage with them in the same way. Annie was always reading, playing pretend, or lying on the couch watching television. Cade had become a serious dancer, and Winnie was very involved with the dance studio. While Don always went to every performance, it wasn't something that he knew how to be involved with on a daily basis. He and Rye shared a special bond. They always had. It was why Rye decided to settle down back home near her parents when she graduated from college. She wanted her children to grow up near both of her parents.

Rye always slept with her phone off. She always believed that she wanted a good night of sleep before receiving bad news. There was no sense in receiving it any earlier than she had to. Rye woke up as usual, walked downstairs to start the coffee pot, and turned on the morning news. She went to go turn on her phone. She had been bracing herself every morning for the text, but had gotten used to only waking up to insignificant work emails over the past couple of days.

This time, she saw there was a text from her mother. She knew what it was going to say. She immediately called Winnie. "When did he pass?" she asked.

"The nurses came in around two in the morning to check on him and he had passed away. He passed in his sleep and didn't feel any pain."

Rye should have felt relief, but she didn't. She felt despair. "Okay," was all she could bring herself to say.

"Oh, Rye, honey, I'm so sorry."

"It's okay, Mom."

"I have to figure out all of the funeral arrangements. I will call you as I figure them out."

Rye couldn't yet wrap her head around going to her father's funeral. She had wanted to be there when her father passed away. She had wanted to be holding his hand. Her father had passed away all by himself. She should have been there.

After work each day, Rye had gone to visit Don in the Hospice home. Every time she set foot into the building, she was nervous they were going to tell her that Don had passed away. She knew this was going to happen eventually, but she wasn't ready yet to hear the words.

It wasn't easy visiting him at the center. The nurses tried to keep him comfortable, but there weren't enough nurses for all of the patients there. She was shocked at the bed he was placed in. He barely fit in it, and she had come one day to find him lying on the floor moaning in pain. He had slid off of his bed and was curled up on the floor unable to pull himself back on the bed. She had called for a nurse, but she had no idea how long he had been left on the floor. It was painful for Rye to see her father this way. The man who cheered lively at the Red Sox, when she hit her first home run, when she made her first basketball shot in a game—lying on the floor completely helpless. Rye wasn't strong enough to pick him up herself.

The last time she had gone to visit, Don looked peaceful. He was resting and had been given enough medication that he wasn't in pain anymore. Don was no longer able to talk breathlessly. He wasn't able to speak at all. Rye would ask him questions, and he would just nod or shake his head. Occasionally, he reached his hand out to hold hers, but that was the extent of their communication. Mostly, Rye sat quietly with him. She brought a book with her, just sitting next to him reading in a chair. Rye just wanted to be near him. Like Winnie, she was nervous he was going to be alone when he did pass, and she wanted to be with him. Don was no longer eating or drinking. She had known it would only be a matter of time.

The rest of the day was a blur. Don had to be moved, and they had to make the funeral arrangements, pick out a coffin, and write an obituary. She was amazed at how much people were expected to do when someone passed away. She could barely think straight, let alone eloquently summarize her father and his life. Rye had to be strong because Winnie had been awake since she received the call at two that morning. It was the first time Winnie had ever asked Rye to drive her anywhere, but she knew that she couldn't drive herself. Rye wasn't sure she was fit to be driving either, but she went to pick up Winnie.

They had called the closest Jewish funeral home. Winnie knew that Don wished to have a traditional Jewish funeral. Rye and Winnie stared at the wide array of caskets. There were so many to choose from. It felt odd putting care into picking out something that was just going to go in the ground for no one to ever see again, yet, at the same time, she wanted her father to have the nicest coffin available. They settled on a pine casket that was simple, but classic, just like Don. Rye was relieved flowers aren't allowed at Jewish funerals, so they didn't have to pick any out.

The funeral home was booked solid. They could have the funeral over the weekend, but there would be other funerals going on at the same time. Winnie wanted a time when Don's would be the only life celebrated, where it would be quiet and peaceful in the funeral home. They would wait until the following Monday. Winnie and Rye both knew it might decrease the number of people who would be able to come, but they didn't want anyone to interfere on the day that was supposed to be only about Don.

Rye drove Winnie back to her house, and they sat to write the obituary together. Neither one of them felt like they had the energy to write it alone. They wrote about his years as a successful doctor and the daughters and grandchildren he was leaving behind. The obituary included only the positives of his life, leaving out the last two years, which weren't really Don. They sent it to Annie and Cade to make sure they were okay with the wording.

Rye left Winnie's house exhausted but knew when she got home she'd be unable to sleep. She would have to put on a brave face for her girls, who would be coming home from school soon. Rye didn't yet have the words to explain to her little girls what had happened. She didn't yet want them to know about death, but she knew that it was inevitable that they were soon to find out. All day,

Rye had focused on the tasks at hand, but now she thought about all her daughters would miss out on losing their grandfather. While he hadn't been himself the last two years, she had still held out hope that someday they'd get to go to a Red Sox game with her father. She had hoped that they would get to watch him cheer.

Annie

High school graduations, moving into college, old trips to the Adirondacks, a vacation to the Grand Canyon, dancing with Annie and Rye at their weddings…all of these memories the three sisters were taping to photo boards that would be hung up at the funeral. Annie had been in charge of bringing most of the photos because Winnie had happened to give her most of the boxes of old pictures when she moved into her condominium with Michael. She brought Avery into the garage in her bassinet. Annie cried and reminisced while Avery kicked her legs in the air. Michael had Nicholas at Rye's house, so he could play with Emilie and Carter while Michael caught up with Will.

All the sisters had composed a piece of writing to share at the funeral. Annie's was a poem. She was known for her poems. She wrote them for every birthday and special occasion, and they were usually humorous. Even this time, Annie was able to add some humor as she remembered her father. He was a human garbage can, and the girls always had to eat quickly, or all of the food would be gone before they could have seconds. Don always made speeches when they were all together that were completely sappy and went on and on. She wrote about these and his genuine love for his family, his work ethic, and his generosity. She was nervous about how she was going to get through reading it, especially in front of a room full of people. Although she was a teacher who stood up in front of middle schoolers on a daily basis when she was working, she was fearful of public speaking. She also wasn't one to talk about her feelings with strangers.

People started trickling in, and Rye grabbed her by the arm and ran into the bathroom.

"I can't do this," Rye cried.

Rye was supposed to be the tough one. She always stayed so strong. "I know," Annie said calmly. "This is going to be really hard, but we will get through it, Rye. We will."

"Just stay here with me, Annie. I don't want to have to talk to anyone."

"Rye, we're going to have to."

Just then, Cade flung the door open. "Where were you guys? I was looking for you everywhere. There are so many people I don't know coming to talk to me about Dad. I can't take it. I need you guys out there with me."

"Can we go out there and all stand together?" Annie asked.

"I can do that," Rye said.

"Me too," added Cade.

They walked out together and stood with one another while people who had known their father came. They were surprised how far some had traveled for their father's funeral. Even his accountant showed up. It was clear that Don had touched many lives, more than they realized, and definitely more than he ever realized. The room was full as they took their seats.

Don's sister was a Rabbi, so she led the service. Annie didn't know what she spoke about because she spent the whole time looking around the room taking in all of the people who had come, all of the people she would have to speak in front of shortly. She pinched her own arm trying to make sure this was all really happening. It felt surreal. Her father was dead. He had come so close over the past two years, but now this was really it. There was no more waiting for the chips to fall. They had finally fallen.

The sisters spoke in birth order. Rye went first, and spoke eloquently about her father. She gave her speech with a shaky voice, but she made it through. Her speech shared beautiful memories and spoke of her father as a hero. It was time for Annie to read her poem. She walked up to the podium after giving Rye a hug and stood there staring out at all the faces. She read her first line and immediately got choked up. She couldn't keep speaking. Annie looked out at the crowd, crying. She looked down at her poem, the lines blurry through her tears. She took a deep breath, spoke into the microphone looking down, and read through her poem. When she finished, she walked back to her seat, Winnie meeting her with a hug. Cade spoke last. It was a sweet speech, but short. Annie knew this had been hard for Cade because her relationship with her father had not always been easy.

The girls stood in a receiving line thanking everyone for coming. It was lunch time, and Annie could feel her stomach growling. Since being on all of the medication, her appetite had increased more than ever before. She just wanted this part to be over. She was sick of saying "thank you" to the strangers who were shaking her hand, telling her how sorry they were for her loss. Michael was watching her from afar, and they locked eyes. She had looked for him after she read her poem to see if he was inside, and she had seen him in the back-rocking Avery back and forth. It turned out that her cousin had taken all of the kids outside and let them run around. She was glad Nicholas hadn't been in the room while she read her poem and broke down in front of the whole room.

After the last person shook her hand, it was time to head to the cemetery. The family decided they would all take one car. They all looked to Rye to drive because she was always the one who knew what to do in every scenario. She was the tough one. It had started to drizzle outside as they walked to the car. As they were walking, Annie saw her father being carried out by a couple of the employees and her mother's brothers. The hearse had been put out in the street with a policeman directing traffic so the procession could begin to the cemetery.

There was a slight chill in the air on that April day, but Annie was sweating in the car. She could feel it dripping down her back. She had never watched anyone be buried before, let alone someone she truly cared about. The drive to the cemetery felt like hours as they drove about twenty miles per hour in the procession. Winnie had warned them that it was surprisingly far from the funeral home, but Annie didn't realize it would feel like they were driving to another state.

Annie wanted Michael. He had taken the kids back to Rye's, which was where people were gathering after the funeral for food. Somehow, Rye had taken care of that too. She really was superwoman sometimes. Annie wanted Michael there to put his arm around her, to give her comfort. Of course, she understood he needed to be with the children, but she needed him too.

They finally pulled into the cemetery and got out of the car. There were chairs in rows, the first row reserved for them. So many people had decided to come to the burial that there was also a circle of people surrounding the chairs. Don's sister explained how the process would work, and said some prayers in Hebrew. The coffin was lowered into the ground and there was a large pile of dirt next to it. Each person would take a scoop of the earth and drop it into the grave. Don's sister warned everyone that the first scoop can be a bit of a shock, and she was right.

Winnie shoveled first. She came back to sit next to Annie, and she was shivering. Annie put her arm around her as Rye went next. Just like they did their speeches in birth order, they buried their father. After they went, other family members scooped dirt and buried their father. The entire family was crying as they sat and watched, holding hands, Annie feeling a squeeze from her mother.

When it was done, they went back to get their own cars and headed to Rye's house. After Annie stuffed her face with food, Rye and Cade barely touching it, they each poured themselves a glass of wine. They had been grieving their father for two years. He had been gone long before this day, and it was time to celebrate his life. Annie decided she would start. She raised her glass towards her sisters, "To Dad," she said.

Rye and Cade raised their glasses as well. "Cheers," they said in unison. They each took a sip of their glass and hugged one another. Annie realized that it was time to start a new chapter. She had worked through the pain of her father and her own life over the past two years, and especially in the last couple of months. It was time to begin anew. This time it would just have to be without her father. Her mother had always said, "This too shall pass." She had been right.

Cade

"Is this because you're Jewish too?"

Cade was getting sick of defending herself, "No," she answered the parent. "It's because there is a separation of church and state. We are not having an Easter party at school."

While Cade enjoyed a celebration, this was where she had to draw the line. Her teaching assistant told her that the parents, grandparents, aunts and uncles were all talking about the fact that she wasn't going to have an Easter party. The students had one when they were in kindergarten, and all of the guardians believed they would be missing out. They all blamed it on Cade being Jewish.

Cade had grown up in the Northeast, and she had gone to public school. An Easter party would never have been allowed. There were too many students in the school who didn't celebrate it. Someone would have gotten offended and called the school. Instead, the school community was offended by her refusal to have an egg hunt, decorate Easter eggs, and take away learning time to celebrate a holy holiday that only certain children in the world celebrated. It didn't seem right, and she was standing firm this time.

She was also mentally and emotionally exhausted from having just come back from her father's funeral. On the plane ride home, Cade had tried to sleep, but she couldn't stop seeing the vision of her father's coffin being lowered in the ground, hearing the sound of the first pile of dirt laid on top by her mother. She had gotten to say her goodbye, but she felt unsettled. There was also a part of her that was dreading going back to North Carolina. Her friends there knew what had happened, but she didn't feel like seeing any of them. Work seemed so daunting, having to pick up the pieces left by a substitute. She didn't have the energy to even get through a morning at Blue River Charter School.

Cade had slept at her mother's house while Annie stayed with Rye. As they stayed up talking, Winnie had said, "Cade, you don't seem like yourself."

"How do you mean, Mom?"

"You don't seem that happy, to be honest, and it's more than just your father dying. I've been thinking this for a while."

"You're right," she cried. "I'm not even sure if I like my friends. I feel like I'm in a teacher boot camp every day, and I'm lonely. Without the idea of Ryan coming to join me, I feel completely alone."

"You know, you don't have to stay there."

"Where would I go? I'll feel like a failure if I just leave."

"You wouldn't be failing, Cade. You would be making a change that was right for you. Why don't you come home?"

"And get a new apartment by myself? Take another chance living with Craigslist roommates? I don't think so. All of my friends have left here and moved on with their lives. I need to too."

"No, honey. Come back here. You can live with me while you figure it all out. Frankly, I could use the company."

Cade thought about this on her way home. She couldn't tell if her mother meant it or was just giving her an out. Winnie had always offered to use herself as an excuse when the girls wanted to get out of something. "Just tell them I said you're not allowed to go," when Cade didn't want to admit that she was scared of downhill skiing and didn't want to go with her friends in middle school. Cade had used the line when her friends were planning a sleepover and everyone was supposed to bring alcohol in water bottles from their houses, but Cade was too afraid to steal her parents' alcohol. Would moving back home solve her problems? Was Winnie asking because she was actually the lonely one? Cade hadn't given her mother a straight answer.

Back at work, the answer became clear to Cade. She had to get out of there, get out of the trenches and to a place where she could breathe. Cade needed to find a place where she belonged, where she wasn't the outcast for her religion or because she didn't want to wear high heels to a barbecue. She was going to go back home. She just needed to tell Ms. Jay.

After school, a few days later, Cade walked along the cement walkway past the other trailers to the main office trailer. She walked straight back through the office, where the two secretaries were separated only by shelving, and back to Ms. Jay's office. It was always a mess in Ms. Jay's office. Books were piled on the floor and on the shelves in all directions. Her desk was always covered with file folders, post-it notes, and loose papers. She didn't know how she ever kept anything organized, but she always seemed to keep the school running as smoothly as possible.

"Oh, Cade! You scared me!" she exclaimed as she looked up in surprise. She had been typing furiously on her computer and didn't see Cade come in.

"Ms. Jay, I need to talk to you about something."

"Cade, I'm so sorry about your father. If you need more time, we can work something out."

"Thank you, but no, it's not that. I have actually decided that I'm going to move back to Connecticut at the end of the year."

"You are? Is there anything we can do to change your mind? You've been such a wonderful addition to Blue River."

"It's not Blue River," Cade partially lied. "I just need to go home and be with my mother for awhile."

"I understand, Cade. Well, know that we are going to miss you greatly. I appreciate you telling me early, so I have time to find someone to replace you for next year, although you won't be easy to replace. I've never seen a teacher work so hard."

It was flattering to hear the words come out of Ms. Jay's mouth. She didn't give compliments often. She was a very kind principal, but she was always talking about the next project or the next initiative. It had, at first, given Cade great anxiety that she would pop into her classroom almost every day. She thought it meant she was in trouble, but she learned it was just what Ms. Jay did. Although the kindergarten teacher had warned her, "If she starts coming in and staying awhile, you're in trouble."

Cade felt like a weight had been lifted off of her shoulders. She knew she still had to make it through June, but there was an end in sight. It was like the treadmill she had been running on was finally turned off. She had no exact plans for her future other than going back home. Maybe she would try to find a teaching job, but after hearing about Rye's experience, she wasn't sure she could work in that extreme either. Her future lay before her, unknown, but inviting.

Winnie

It is Jewish tradition that a year after the burial, the headstone is placed upon the grave. This tradition, known as the unveiling, is an intimate moment shared only by the closest family and friends. Winnie agonized over the wording of the headstone. Don's sister had given Winnie the Hebrew translation of his name to include, and Winnie had sent multiple emails to her daughters asking for their opinion on what to write. They had finally concluded with, "Loving Husband and Father, Dedicated Compassionate Physician." Rye had helped Winnie make the final decision to switch the order, as Winnie had put "physician" first. While Don had spent most of his life devoted to his work, at times over his family, Rye felt that his life as a father and husband should be remembered first.

The next day, sitting on the Adirondack chairs, Winnie marveled at her beautiful family and the backdrop of the Adirondack mountains surrounded by blue skies and few clouds. The porch looked down over Lake George, glistening in the sunlight. They had just come back from a boat ride. Nicholas, Emilie, and Carter had gotten to drive the boat. Don would have loved seeing the pure joy on their faces and the picturesque scenery that surrounded them as they zoomed around the lake.

Rye felt it best to commemorate a year passing of their father's death at the Adirondacks. The last two years there brought back a flood of negative emotions, but it was a place where Don had previously felt alive. It was a place where they shared memories at the beach, on the boats, running through the fields, getting ice cream at the ice cream shop, and hiking in the mountains.

They went on a family hike, not as steep as they had done with Don because Nicholas, Emilie, and Carter were too little, but with Avery asleep in a hiking backpack, they had completed a one-mile hike as a family. When they reached the top of the summit, the whole family took a picture with the mountains across the lake behind them, setting up the camera on a rock. It was hard to get the grandchildren to sit still, but they captured the moment when they all were remembering their father, only the good parts.

Annie was back to herself and back at work. She was still on a cocktail of medications, and she still saw Dr. Ruman every three months. When Winnie talked to Annie about it, Annie expressed how badly she wanted to get off of the medications, but it wasn't yet the right time. Avery, thankfully, continued to be an easy child. She was now a toddler, and although they were growing out of their condominium, for the time being, her life was settled.

Cade had moved back home and into Winnie's house. She had taken a break from teaching for a while and was tutoring local children. In Fairfield County, Connecticut, this meant an income of over one hundred dollars an hour for some families. She was making significantly more money than she had when she was at Blue River Charter School, working about half of the time, but her health insurance was expensive. However, her stress level had greatly decreased.

Rye was still doing it all. She had organized the trip to the Adirondacks, and she was still teacher of the year in Winnie's eyes, even though she hadn't been nominated that year. She didn't talk to Winnie much about her feelings since Don had passed. Occasionally, she made comments like "Dad would have loved to see this," or "too bad Dad isn't here to enjoy this." Winnie thought maybe she had forgotten about the past two years and meant his life before that, because over the past two years, Don hadn't enjoyed anything. Rye was the only one who had held onto hope through it all, so the loss was most devastating to her. She did mention offhandedly that she was seeing a therapist, so Winnie was glad she was talking to someone, even if it wasn't to her.

Winnie's biggest surprise was that life didn't change that much, except that she now had to refer to herself as a "widow." She still attended the caregivers' group in order to offer support to the other members, and she still gathered with her spiritual group to support her. She kept up her volunteering, lunches with her neighbors, and nights out to the theater. She had even joined a meditation group where she had met a man she'd been talking to every night. She didn't tell her girls yet, because she didn't know if they'd think that it was too soon. For Winnie, she had grieved the loss of Don long before he finally passed. For her, it was the first time she felt relief for him and for herself having to look after him. She was experiencing a new sense of freedom that she hadn't had in two years. For once, she wasn't waiting for the next crisis, for the next chip to fall.

Nicholas, Emilie, and Carter were kicking around a ball on the field as Avery toddled around, having just learned to walk a couple of months earlier. She walked over to Avery and swooped her up into her arms holding her close, singing softly into her ear. Still holding Avery, Winnie felt the ball roll into her foot, and she kicked the ball as hard she could towards Nicholas. Her daughters were sitting on a blanket in the grass, chatting away, but too far for Winnie to hear what they were talking about. She inhaled the fresh Adirondack air and breathed, remembering not to take her breath for granted.

About The Author

Rebecca Hendrickson is a special education teacher at an alternative high school in Fairfield County, Connecticut. She resides in Norwalk, Connecticut with her husband and two children. She previously published *The Four Trimesters: Poems Highlighting the Joys of Motherhood,* which can be found on Amazon. Writing has always been her creative outlet, and *Lessons from the Mountain* is her first work of fiction.